Unjani Mfwethu?

The story of a migrant in South Africa

Ayodeji Olaifa

DEDICATION

To Yety, Fikun and David,
you are my world.

To all migrants everywhere,
may you find light in the dark.

Copyright © 2021 Ayodeji Olaifa
Unjani Mfwethu?
The story of a migrant in South Africa

Published by Bonani Contents (Pty) Ltd
Cape Town, South Africa
For publishing queries or general information please visit our website
www.bonanicontents.com

Edited by Amy Raynard
Cover design by Molebogeng Setlaelo

ISBN 978-0-620-92958-5

All rights reserved.
No part of this book may be reproduced, stored in a retrieval system or transmitted in any form or by any means of electronic, mechanical, photocopying, recording, scanning, or by any other information storage or retrieval system, without prior written permission from the publisher or author.

CONTENTS

PROLOGUE.. 6

CHAPTER 1 - The Rude Awakening............. 10

CHAPTER 2 - Leaving my Country............... 37

CHAPTER 3 - Unmasking the Country....... 59

CHAPTER 4 - The Break of Dawn................. 98

CHAPTER 5 - Homecoming............................ 123

EPILOGUE... 162

PROLOGUE

Sanibonani!

Humans, since earliest times have been on the move. Some for economic reasons, some to study, some to join families and some fleeing from sexual or other forms of abuse. Others move because they have been displaced by conflict. There are few who may not even know why they are on the move – but would just move anyway.

Humans achieve greatness when they are able to harness the power of community and partnerships. This is called Ubuntu in South Africa - I am because you are. It refers to the practice of building and restoring humanity. This is even more crucial in the life of a migrant. To survive is to unite in thoughts, goals, and efforts. Every day in the life of the migrant is a new struggle, a new aspiration, a new hope and yet, more of the old, the norm. It can sometimes be a life in perpetual migration!

Among the many things that migrants share, storytelling is perhaps the most influential. Migrants feed off stories – real or unreal, and sometimes in between. These stories quickly evolve into strong opinions and arguments traversing all imaginable topics and lasting many days. Storytelling is an act of communion. It brings people together regardless of their differences - physical or social.

These stories usually revolve around the successes and failures of other migrants, the do's, and don'ts of the new land. Stories serve as both sources of entertainment and education. It is in the stories that migrants find hope. Stories provide the strength to hold on to the promise of the new land, to believe in the hospitality of your new hosts. Stories help migrants build homes far away from home. In fact, stories, no matter how 'incredulous', are the eyes and ears of 'foreigners' in a world about which very little is known but are keen to explore.

After all, storytelling is life and life is storytelling!

It was sometime in April 2002. I had just arrived in South Africa a few weeks earlier. We were all cramped together in our shared apartment in Sunnyside, Pretoria. I was working for a cosmetic company, in a network marketing structure. Some of my friends also worked in the same company. As I am regularly reminded, I was lucky to have found a job barely days after I arrived in the country. It can take months and sometimes years to obtain a job as a foreigner. I was truly grateful.

An argument ensued over one of the many stories flying around in the gathering. It was about a lifestyle survey that some of my friends were involved in, and this time, I couldn't withhold my astonishment. There is absolutely no way that it could be right! How could anyone be earning R40, 000 per month? Did he have his own business perhaps? There must have been a mistake somewhere. He probably meant it as an annual salary! My friend Dominique was insistent. He argued that he was just as flabbergasted as I am when he saw the figures.

He repeatedly asked the respondent at the Engen garage in Waterkloof, (one of Pretoria's rich suburbs) if the figures provided were correct. The respondent was a middle-aged white male, employed in the financial services industry, and was earning just above R40, 000 per month. I thought to myself that something just did not seem right. It was easier to believe that my friend, once again, was guilty of embellishment.

A monthly salary of just over R3000 was more acceptable to my little mind in 2002. My monthly income during this time was R600 - out of which I had to pay a monthly rent of R400. It was absolutely impossible to conceive a monthly earning of such magnitude! There are just somethings that a 'captured mind' is unable to fathom, no matter how hard one tries. My world at that moment was one that could only be dreamt of.

Dominique is one of many migrants in the country who had worked with this marketing company prior to joining the cosmetic company. They were employed to conduct lifestyle income surveys across the country. The survey was usually conducted in affluent suburbs and malls across the country. It was designed to qualify individuals by income levels, with the promise of a holiday getaway voucher.

The real intention behind the survey was of course, to sell travel packages and financial services products to the selected candidates. However, this was never disclosed upfront. From the marketing company's perspective, foreigners are better suited for such tasks. They would be grateful for any form of lifeline in a country that offers them little or no opportunities, especially those from the rest of the continent.

CHAPTER 1
The Rude Awakening

It was the middle of May 2002. The beginning of winter was already starting to bite hard in Pretoria. Dominique and I had trouble getting ready for work, particularly on this day. It had been a long night. Our landlord, Serikit, an old German lady, who believed that she was at least 20 years younger than her biological age, had again kept us up with her usual tantrums. Dominque had failed to clean the stove and the bathtub earlier in the day and now we had to endure hours of tongue-lashing and threats of eviction. Thabo, the 16-year-old boyfriend, stood there gloating. He had never been a fan of my roommate and had vowed to get rid of him and us, technically speaking. Our saving grace, however, was the greed of his girlfriend. She just could not let go of the tax-free rental income she was getting every month. It was too much trouble trying to find new tenants. We were secure for the moment.

My phone rang and it was our colleague and friend, Ola, calling to check if we were on our way to the office. The office was a makeshift place in the backyard of a Sunnyside studio. I am not sure what arrangements our employer, Mark, a white British South African, had with the property owners. However, we were always welcomed at the premises no matter the hour. I remember picking up my first 'Kwaito' steps during the many parties we attended at this spot after closing work.

Dominque and I arrived a little after 08:00. It always infuriated me to be late. Ola was already seated, and we proceeded to our respective 'territories'. Ola and I were allocated to Pretoria East for the quarter, and Dominque had the entire Pretoria West to himself. He just seemed to enjoy working alone and getting lost in the solitude of the dusty roads along the industrial town. Ola and I could never understand him.

I particularly liked working in Pretoria East. The views were a sharp contrast to what I was used to in the central part of the city. Pretoria was my first home in South Africa. I had arrived earlier in the year in March 2002. I was picked up by friends from OR Tambo International Airport and from there, went straight to a church function at Rhema Church somewhere in Randburg. They apologized for not taking me home directly and hoped that I would enjoy the service. The huge auditorium was filled to capacity. I remember being mesmerized at the sheer size of the church. The flamboyance reminded me of churches I had left behind in Nigeria.

Something in my mind told me that things were going to be all right. It had to be. South Africa, from the little I could see - the airport, the highways, and churches - looked picturesque compared to where I was coming from. I was starting to feel good about my decision. Little did I know that I would come to rely so much on that early burst of positivity that I felt.

I spent two days in Johannesburg and was reunited with my old-time friend from back home, Dominique, in Sunnyside Pretoria. Sunnyside was predominantly a student area. The town exuded so much energy. It was a melting pot of some sort. The ideal place for a newcomer to get into the heart of the city and country almost immediately, although Johannesburg ranks higher in that respect. In addition to the student population, one could not miss the ever-increasing presence of African foreigners beside other locals. Some were working in the Central Business District (CBD) and others trying to survive just like the rest of the foreigners. There were also a handful of Asians and Westerners hustling in the neighbourhood. By the time I arrived in 2002, I was told that majority of the white South Africans had moved further away into the suburbs. The few local whites around were either day visitors looking for 'fixes' or those that were too poor to move. No one really noticed.

Old Pretoria East, Hatfield and Brooklyn, is an upstate part of Pretoria. The University of Pretoria is situated in Hatfield, with its rich history and colourful grounds. My friends and I would always retire to the campus vicinity after each day's work to relax and enjoy some of the view. It reminded us of our campus days back home. I missed the vibe so much. I started to imagine getting back into the groove, except it would be a different groove this time. I would have to work to fund my studies. Brooklyn, on the other side of the road, was a mix of thriving small businesses. It included big corporate offices, embassies, residential homes as well as a beehive of high-end entertainment spots - not the type we could afford.

That morning, Mark reminded us of changes to the business. Our commission on each bottle of perfume sold was going to be increased from R25 to R35. It was great news! Serikit had been complaining about delays in the payment of our rent. She threatened to impose fines on late payments going forward. I had always resisted the temptation to ask, in between her long stories about how she escaped from America and having stolen millions from her ex-husband and eventually arriving in South Africa and investing all her stolen wealth in the stock market, why a few days delay in rent gave her such sleepless nights. But then, I understand the power of greed.

Alighting from the car, I bade farewell to Ola for the day

as he made his way to the Brooklyn area and I proceeded further on foot towards the residential suburbs of the East. The topography of the 'Kloof' areas of Pretoria East are just breath-taking! Even though the popular Jacaranda trees were by now a ghost of its beautiful self, it was still a dream to walk those beautiful streets with huge trees. Later I came to understand, the presence of trees is a sign of a wealthy suburb - never mind the heavy bag I was carrying all the way.

Street Hawking is both an art and a science.

Choosing your first target is never an easy task. It is a very strategic exercise involving a variety of hunting skills. The prioritisation of targets, approach, and eventual kill, are skills that are sharpened over time with experience. It is the ability to stare at a bold sign that reads "No Hawkers Allowed" and proceed to press the buzzer without blinking, that determines who survives and who does not.

Office complexes are often more attractive, given the relatively higher concentration of potential clients. However, they can also be as tight as a bank vault to break into. The benefits often outweigh the risks. If successful, it is a territory that could be worked on for weeks and months. It is no different from a producing mine. Next to the office complexes, are shopping malls. Yes, shopping malls! It is one of the ironies of life. Many of those who work in some of those high-end beauty and retail stores, may not be able to afford the products sold in those stores. That is where we come in to serve. Shopping malls have similar security challenges, if not even more difficult than office complexes, given that mall security systems are more complex.

There are often many security personnel wandering around the entire mall. Precision and speed are highly required in working within the malls. Our targets are often our black brothers and sisters who would congregate at different spots at the delivery sections of the malls. These are also blind spots for the security people. Other good territories include, but not limited to, petrol stations, auto shops and dealerships, government departments as well as, home/office hybrids that are common on the main streets of suburbs.

These spots provide opportunities for quick sales but without the volumes, you would expect in other territories. It also helps that we have a good product that serves a crucial need given that many consumers are unable to afford the relatively more expensive 'luxury items', a less expensive 'look–alike' version of these goods present an attractive opportunity. This industry has grown exponentially in recent times and representing a multibillion-dollar market.

"How are you bro?" I gestured to the security guy at the Castle Walk office complex in Erasmuskloof. "Unjani?" he replied. That is often when the relationship starts to go south. As soon as I am unable to respond in any of the local languages. "I am fine bro" I uttered back, noticing that his countenance immediately changed. "I have a meeting here," I continued. He looked at me suspiciously whilst staring at my handbag full of perfume testers. I told him that I was meeting with an Annalie Strydom. Mark had trained us on the art of random name-dropping. It worked again! Before I was let in, my brother fumed. "Bhuti, can you not speak Zulu? Are you not a black person?" I was perplexed. "Sorry man, not every black person is Zulu!" I muttered some words in my native language and I could hear him shouting as I made my way to the office blocks. He definitely got the message. It was a bad attempt on my side. I know better not to make enemies of security personnel. They are the ones between me and my rent!

I had to quickly decide on which block to attack first, given that the security guy was most likely watching my every movement. I walked into the first office block I set my eyes on and hoped that it would not be like some other office complexes with different levels of security - just when you think you have escaped the man at the main gate, you are confronted with yet another at the entry post of each individual offices. On this day, it appeared that the stars were aligned in my favour. The only security I could see through the transparent door was a young white lady sitting behind the reception desk. I breathed a huge sigh of relief, pressed the intercom and again, like a good omen, the kind lady buzzed me in without much fuss.

Every stage in the selling process requires a different skillset. As much as the security personnel are perhaps one of the toughest obstacles to our business, receptionists, or front desk personnel, are no pushovers either. One wrong move, and the 'Mr can you not speak Zulu?' would be summoned immediately to throw me out! Front desks are more vulnerable to appearances. Hence, it is for moments like this that Mark had insisted on a dress code. I thought it was ridiculous to expect us to wear dress shoes in our line of work, given the kilometres we cover every day on foot. We had to compromise given that he had demanded a full corporate look. I just could not see myself in a shirt and tie selling perfumes on the street. It was simply ridiculous. I thought I looked presentable enough in my slowly growing afro, which I planned to make into dreadlocks and, my casual shirts with a pair of jeans and comfortable shoes. This is South Africa after all! Everyone was flashing Converse shoes or 'All Star Tekkies', as popularly known in the country. I needed to fit in. It took a while to understand that there was another rational behind his suggestion of a corporate look. Apparently, it was in our best interest as young black men walking around predominantly white suburbs and businesses, to not fall into the trap of stereotype.

The lady smiled and asked how she could be of help. Like a predator, I looked around the office quickly taking in the layout. If I could see the inner offices from the front desk or not. With her permission, I put down my briefcase on her desk and swiftly unzipping the bag to let out the bait - the sweet aroma of oil based French perfumes. Not allowing her much time to recover, I got straight into my pitch. "Thank you again for letting me in. I do not plan to waste any of your time. I am here to show you and your colleagues some beautiful French perfumes that we have on special". Like a professional magician, before she was able to read the usual riot act, I unpacked the testers while the room continue to soak in the beautiful fragrance of the perfumes. I sprayed one of our finest on a paper and handed it to her for approval. It was very hard to resist such temptation. This is the point where, depending on how formal the office is, I am invited into a meeting room or the front desk is converted into an exhibition hall for the entire duration of my pitch.

Unjani Mfwethu?

On this day, we chose the latter. The front desk lady was hypnotized. It turned out she was a perfume expert, reeling different French names off her sleeve. Thankfully, I had most of her favourites on display. She wanted to test as many as possible. I cautioned against testing more than three of four. Even my coffee beans at that stage, would be of little help in clearing the smell for the next and she was impressed. I had my first sale for the day. She ordered a 50ml bottle of Red Door by Elizabeth Arden. Thankfully, I had stock on me, so I wrote a receipt and handed her the bottle. Mark had implored us to use our discretion. The goal was not to return stocktaking. Do whatever it takes to push a sale but do not lose a bottle. We were solely responsible for every bottle taken out. Selling or buying goods on credit, was quite new to me. This was not a usual practice in Nigeria at the time. Nigeria was a cash economy. It was arguably the true hallmark of a less developed economy. You bought consumer goods on a cash on delivery basis, at least for most people. Worthy to note that in the space of about a decade when I returned home, I was very surprised to see all manners of payment schemes being pushed down the consumer's throat.

The best part of a first sale is that the buyer now becomes an agent without knowing it. The agent unconsciously, expands the territory even more so, as he or she goes about spreading the good news. It was exactly what was happening. Now my new convert, whom I now know to be Anne, based on the issued receipt, called out to her colleagues to join the party. "You can buy now and pay on the 25th" she sang out to her colleagues. I nodded in agreement with the smile of a successful hunt. There is something assuring about a group of white middle age women salivating over a product, especially one being sold by a black person. I could smell additional sales and it felt very good. I had a feeling this was where I would most likely end the day's business. What a pick!

I have always been a fan of Mariah Carey. I selected her greatest hit CD from the stack of CDs at the R&B section at Musica in Brooklyn mall and settled in comfortably into one of listening booths. I felt a vibration in my right pocket. It was Ola calling. He was also done for the day and was wondering where I was. He agreed to meet me at Musica. He is an avid lover of everything music and could not pass on an opportunity to listen to some music as well. Musica stores was an essential service to many.

I remember a story told of a fellow migrant and friend. Jaden lived in Johannesburg. Like many foreigners again, African foreigners, in South Africa at the time, Jaden was employed in the burgeoning private security industry. The security companies would recruit, train, and deploy security personnel, armed or unarmed, to various businesses across the country. Jaden was an unarmed security personnel. His salary was decent by any measure, earning an average of about R900 monthly. It was much more stable in comparison to the commission we earned in the perfume business. It thus, attracted more people who preferred the stability. As to be expected, a cartel quickly developed and controlled the recruitment process of foreigners for these security companies.

Typically, you would be introduced to an agent of the cartel, who would arrange for the leasing of an unarmed security license within the network. The same agent will also arrange for your employment at a security company. You would therefore become an imposter. Payroll is aligned and salaries are deposited into the original license holders bank account provided by the agent. The cartel also ensured that you receive your due share net of all fees. I guess one could therefore argue that the net salary of a security personnel in this case, may not be better than what we earned as street hawkers. Perhaps it boiled down to the preference for stability and less trekking all over town.

Jaden was allocated to an abandoned construction site within a walking distance of the East Gate Mall in Johannesburg.

According to legends, Jaden would report to the construction site early in the morning and would immediately make his way to the mall where he would spend hours at Musica listening to assorted and free music all day. Who needed to buy musical CDs if you could listen to an array of music all day, for free, in a private booth with state-of-the-art gadgets!

The day Jaden lost his job was like any other day. There was no drama, no special premonition. He did not stump his left foot on the way to work. It was just a regular day. Jaden arrived at work as usual at 08:00 that fateful day. He completed his 20-minute routine site inspection and as usual, reported to Musica. He quickly settled into the legendary song 'No Woman, No Cry' by Bob Marley, a remix by Lauren Hill. Call it fate or ill luck, but his day was about to get very rocky. Jaden's boss walked into the store looking to pick up a few Afrikaaner musical CDs. Watching as he struggled to make up his mind, a friendly attendant suggested that he sit at one of the music booths to sample a few of the CDs. Yes, the boss chose the booth right opposite Jaden, who was by now lost in the music. Jaden then joined our perfume business but based out of Johannesburg. As testament to his unbeatable work ethics, he consistently won the annual prize for the best salesperson nationally in the company for three years in a row.

Unjani Mfwethu?

Again, my phone started vibrating vigorously. It was Ola trying to let me know that he was at the mall and would rather wait outside. I got up from the booth, hung up the bogus headset and made my way to the exit. We both made our way to the food court, picked a free bench in the middle of the food court, and settled down to recount the events of the day. Food courts were only a chilling spot for us. We only ate home cooked meals, not because it was healthier but because it was wiser. I still maintain the same perspective today albeit, broader.

Ola had a good day. He made a few sales for the day. There have been many days without a single sale. I tried not to show my excitement, but it was hard to suppress. Even though I did not make any cash sales on the day, I sold twelve bottles on credit. Anne had bought one bottle and her two friends had bought four bottles each. She had also walked with me to the next office block, with 'Mr can you not speak Zulu' and helped me secure three additional orders. It was a record setting day. My rent was assured for the month. Ola was impressed. We sent an SMS to Mark advising him that we were ready to be picked up outside the Brooklyn Mall. It was time to gather back at the office and account for the days sales and plan for the big day.

I had just loaded the R25 credit voucher that I bought during the day. It was time to send SMS reminders to my clients ahead of the big deliveries. Cash on deliveries were 90% of our total sales and the remainder, usually split between instant cash sales or credit sales for future dated payments. This month has been particularly kind to me. My earlier deliveries on the 15th and 21st went relatively smooth with less than 30% cancellations. Many would develop a buyer's remorse minutes after placing their order and would call to cancel - sometimes even before you have left the premises. Interestingly, we encountered higher cancellation numbers among our black brothers and sisters probably because majority of their orders are in fact sympathy orders. They just seemed to want to support us even when their budgets could not support it. The bold ones would call to cancel while the less bold would become evasive. We always preferred the bold ones, saves everyone unnecessary hassles. Whatever the case, we were just grateful for the support provided by all. As time went on, we learnt to make provisions for this in our projected monthly earnings. I was quite excited about the next morning's prospects. Even Serikit noticed my unusually upbeat mood as I went about doing the evening chores in the flat without the usual grumblings. Life or maybe cash, is good!

I arrived early at Castle Walk office complex feeling more

familiar now. I did not have to lie about my intentions to the security guard this time. It was a different person at the gate. I miss my friend 'Mr can you not speak Zulu'. I nodded to the security guy and said hello. He responded in English. I suspected that he was a foreigner like me, given he did not make any fuss about speaking Zulu or Sesotho.

Anne buzzed me in with a smile. That was a good sign. Delivery days are usually very busy as we had to cover as many grounds as quickly as possible before lunch time, to avoid clients blowing their salaries on all sorts of shopping extravaganza before we arrive. Thus, we tend to keep the 'chit chats' as short as possible on delivery days. I did the basic pleasantries and brought out my sales book. I was owed payment for twelve bottles in the complex. Anne was professional. She immediately took out her copy of the sales receipt and paid me R100. I asked for the other two ladies, Joelen and Bekker. I noticed a bit of hesitation and wondered why but she reached for the desk phone anyway. She told Joelen I was in the office. I reminded her of Bekker. With the same slight hesitation, I had noticed few seconds ago, she told me Bekker had resigned with immediate effect. She stopped work a few days ago.

I was a little confused because I sent her an SMS even though she did not respond. Why did she not tell me that she had resigned? Alarm bells started to ring in my ears. I cannot afford any delay in payment. She already has the bottles. My thoughts were interrupted by Joelen's arrival and immediately, she handed the R300 to me. I was momentarily pleased even though the shock of Bekker's resignation was still evident on my face. Anne was quick to bring the ladies up to speed. I instinctively took out my phone and called her. She did not answer. I called again... voice mail. My face dropped! Four bottles! This was not happening!

When you lose a bottle of perfume, you not only lose your commission, but you are also liable for the cost of the bottle. Mark had no time for excuses. He never believed in them. He once made us huge posters explaining why excuses were for losers. We understood that he was running a business and despite of his white privilege, he was a street hustler. He had managed to put some funds together to purchase a franchise and we were just grateful that he gave us the opportunity to earn a living. I did the math. Losing four bottles was the equivalent of the total commission on eleven bottles, which was about two third of my average monthly income. I was devastated!

As saddened as I was, I knew I had other deliveries to make. I picked up my bag and made my way to the next block to deliver the remaining three bottles. Thankfully, there was no

Unjani Mfwethu?

drama. My client kindly left the money in an envelope with the front desk lady. I gave her the bottles and picked up my money. I checked again to see if she had changed her mind about the perfume, but she was still adamant. She thought for a moment and suggested that she could give me a referral to a friend across the road. She reiterated that she was not promising anything. I gave her a 15ml complimentary bottle, reassuring her that I understood and that I would give it a shot. To me, it was more than just a shot. Referrals provided unlimited access to buildings. I started to feel a little better. Maybe I might just be able to recover some of the day's losses. Who knows!

Tshepo was exceptionally warm for a black South African. I liked him immediately. Nigerian and South African males do not always hit it off at the first instance – there had been too many stories flying around between the two groups. I waited for almost an hour at the reception of the gigantic SITA building. I had time to burn anyway. I was done with my deliveries for the day and was hoping for a good omen. SITA seemed to be the ideal target. I watched as droves of young professionals, black, white and brown males and females, walked up and down the escalator.

Michelle, the receptionist, apologized to me again and

reassured that Tshepo would soon be back. He usually took extended lunch breaks. While waiting, it occurred to me that I should show her what I had in my bag. However, on a second thought, I did not think it was a good idea. There was just too much activity going on in the big reception area. I chose to just enjoy the view and dream, while I waited for Tshepo.

Finally, he arrived. Tshepo ensured that I had a visitor tag, and we made our way to one of the meeting rooms. He confirmed that Bokang, the lady that referred me, already gave him the heads up. I showed him what I was selling and asked what his favourite fragrance was. He smiled and asked if I had Paco by Paco Rabanne. It was a good choice. We called the look alike 'Cuba'. He smelt it and liked it. Immediately, he placed an order for two bottles. He scanned the remaining items on the list with urgency and ordered three more male fragrances. He asked about the logistics and we agreed for cash on delivery for the next payment date, 25th of June.

I did not know what to make of the experience at all. It was a pleasant meeting. I did not know if I should trust the orders placed, or not. It was a good thing that it was not a credit sale. I would not be too disappointed if it turned out to be another cancelled order. I laughed at myself as I remembered my desperate attempt at securing a pitch with his colleagues. He had nicely declined and told me that we should rather plan for another time. I thanked him and made my way out to the reception hall. The 25th was racking up pleasantly. I already secured another sale at the Castle office complex with Jolene's friend, Monica.

Michelle was not on seat. I think I am good for the month's rent. It was not a bad month despite the hiccups and scam of the day. I had a hunch to try Bekker's phone again, hiding my caller ID. It rang a few times. I thought I heard a voice, so I shouted, "hello!" I heard a beep and again, voice mail. It was time to call Ola.

Sunday is my Sabbath day. I usually start the day at a predominantly Nigerian church in the CBD and thereafter, enjoy a marathon of movies at the Ster-Kinekor in Acadia. It did not take long for me to be awarded a platinum movie card, which came with many benefits including express service at the counters. Sometimes after my round of movies, I would meet up with friends at Kruger Park - where Ola stayed or I would just go home to prepare for the week ahead, if Serikit would permit.

That Sunday was not very restful. I was woken up to Serikit's agonising grunts in the apartment. It was one of her ways of getting attention. The moment she heard my door open, she came barging towards me. "Oh Babyface, (that is the pet name she gave me), I do not know what to do. I can't get Thabo to Germany. The mama will not give me his birth certificate", she ranted in her strong German accent. She said Thabo's mum had threatened to have her arrested. Now she had my full attention! Nothing rattles foreigners more than the thought of the police snooping around their nests.

Even though I tried hard to avoid being in her room, I ushered her there to avoid early morning drama with Dominique who was still deeply asleep. Once we were in her room, I asked her to tell me the full story, while trying to keep my eyes off the despicable nude pictures of Thabo plastered all over her wall.

Thabo was a kid from Soweto who like many, had ended up on the streets of Sunnyside, Pretoria. He had been in and out of prison frequently for petty crimes and would always end up on the streets. Serikit remembered him as one of the street kids she regularly provided food and clothes to, as part of her way to redeem herself from her previous life in the States. The prison staff told her that he was in prison for failing to raise a R200 bail. Serikit quickly increased her home bond to

Unjani Mfwethu?

bail him out of prison. Thabo henceforth become her lover. She told herself that he was 21 years old.

For reasons best known to her, she decided that she wanted to take him overseas. The first step of course was getting Thabo a travel document. Expectedly, Thabo did not have an ID document and therefore needed to retrieve his birth certificate to apply for both an ID and an International Passport. They decided to make a trip to Zululand in Kwa-Zulu Natal, to meet his mum. She thought that this might be a great opportunity to meet Thabo's family. Obviously, the meeting in Natal did not go as she wished. She was not happy seeing an older white woman in the arms of her young child, and threatened to open a case of statutory rape with the police. It appeared that Serikit was only able to 'escape' as a free woman - with Thabo left behind - after a mutually beneficial contract was agreed. I did not know how to console her. I had never been in support of the relationship, even though I never had any issues with Thabo personally. If at all, I enjoyed his stories on the socio-political and economic evolution of crime in South Africa. I hugged her and told her I was late for church. I spent more time at the cinema on this day. I was not looking forward to going home.

On a painfully cold morning in June, I received a surprise call from Tshepo. He wanted to know if I could deliver his bottles earlier. Great news! Perhaps I may be able to replace my old leather jacket after all with a more appropriate winter jacket. I called Mark and asked if he had stock available. I told him it was an early delivery. Thankfully, he had stock available. I made my way to his commune in Gerard Murdherk Sunnyside, where I picked up the bottles and darted off to Erasmuskloof via Walker Street.

I said hello to Michelle and asked to see Tshepo. She gave me my pass and directed me to the waiting area. I almost did not recognize him as he walked towards me. He had a big plaster across his face and looked quite tired. He gestured for me to come with him to a private meeting room. He apologized for interrupting my schedule. He had some window in his budget and thought he should not hold me for longer. I thanked him and gave him the bottles, all the time, still staring at his face hoping for some explanation. Rather, he wanted to follow up on a conversation about my personal life... what I was doing besides selling perfumes.

We spoke about Nigeria and my plans to enrol for a postgraduate programme in marketing at the University of South Africa (UNISA). He said he was proud. He asked if we could make his order a recurring one for the remainder of the year. With a surprised but delightful look, I made out a recurring receipt for two bottles of Cuba for the next six months and handed it over to him. "No, no", he said. "I want the same five bottles starting from this month, the 25th". I was shell-shocked! I asked why he was ordering so many. He laughed. He told me it was not for him, but he plans to give them out to some of his friends and younger men in his neighbourhood. Moreover, he reckons this could support in some way, my plans for further studies.

He narrated his story to me. How tough it was growing up and how his mum had to literally work herself to death to fund his and the sibling's education. He told me he still lives in the same family house, now tastefully renovated. He could not bear to leave all the memories especially since the passing of his mum. He always told himself never to join the 'migration' of successful black professionals to the white suburbs, as was the case with many in the townships. He would rather stay and be actively involved in the upliftment of his community and be an inspiration to younger kids.

However, all of that may be in jeopardy, at least the part of staying back in the township. Tshepo was attacked on his way home and ironically, by some of the people he was trying to inspire. He encountered many lacerations across the face and all for a mere cell phone and an empty wallet. He was lucky to be alive. Crime was exploding by the day across South African townships. Too many young lives cut short and rape crimes spiralling out of control. He asked rhetorically, "can you blame anyone for moving away to the suburbs, to safety - even if it is just an illusion?"

Tshepo's story would remain with me for a while. I remember as Thabo had told me about the nature of crime in South Africa, in his own opinion. Criminals had started stealing from the suburbs and the foreigners or tourists. He mentioned that some of the black policemen and the community, would turn a blind eye and would in many ways suggest to them that 'it was okay to take back what was taken from them originally'. I guess what the community did not envisage was that the same criminals would soon turn to their own communities causing unstoppable havoc. How do you reign in a criminal that you once nurtured?

Tshepo is an extraordinary South African! He showed me, in many ways, how to be kind and how to rise above prejudices. He epitomizes the spirit of Ubuntu! He showed me the power of kindness.

On 25 June, I made my way to Erasmuskloof. Thankfully,

Unjani Mfwethu?

Mark was kind enough to drop Ola and I off at Brooklyn mall. We had quite several deliveries for the day, which makes him a happy man. My idea of sending a SMS reminder had magically transformed the business. Cancellations on delivery days had reduced significantly and I, was duly rewarded with five 15ml sample bottles.

I dropped off Tshepo's orders with Michelle and picked up my cash. I knew he would be unavailable on the day according to his response to my SMS the previous night. He had instructed that I pick up my money at the front desk. On my way to the Castle Walk office complex, I stopped midway at the Engen garage to deliver a bottle and managed to get another order for the following month. When I reached the Castle Walk complex, I noticed 'Mr. Zulu' was on shift and so, decided to humour him. I shouted 'Sanibonani' across the gate and told him that I had an appointment with Monica. He cracked a smile and waved me on. I made a note to practice my linguistic skills more. Perhaps I should try showing him some samples to or, maybe not.

I saw Anne outside the office block smoking a cigarette. We made small talks for few minutes and I asked if Monica was available. I had to pick up the payment for the two bottles she had picked up the previous month. What happened next set my heart into race mode. I do not know what it was exactly - whether it was her cigarette accidently burning her finger in a frantic move or the stare she gave, like someone who had just seen a ghost! Her face immediately went red when she asked if I did not get paid on the day, I gave her the bottles. I sat down on the curb and looked her in the eye. I asked to know what was going on. She revealed that Monica had left the company some weeks back, apparently just after I was in their office. I took out my receipt book, my phone, and dialled her. After a few rings, she came online. I told her I was at her workplace and Anne just told me she is no longer working there. I asked her if there was a place, I can meet with her to pick up my money?

The challenge with trading or working 'under the table' is that you often have very little or no recourse to law enforcement. In fact, you get threatened with law enforcement regularly by scums disguising as decent people. When in truth all they are, are low-life scums who just want to steal from you. In such cases, you are better off just walking away and hope for better times. That was exactly my reaction when Monica told me unequivocally on the phone to never call her phone again or she would send the police after me! It felt like I had just taken a hard blow to my jaw, one that would leave me unconscious for a long while!

CHAPTER 2
Leaving my Country

As we all sat together in the family room just a few days prior to my 29th birthday, I went through my boxes again for the umpteenth time with my siblings. It was my first time flying. It was a day I had dreamt of, countless times, and each time I have had to accompany my girlfriend to the airport. This time was different. I was the one leaving. I honestly did not think it would take this long to happen.

I arrived at the airport hours before my scheduled flight. You just never know what to expect with Lagos traffic as well as the notorious airport immigration officials. The check-in process went quite smoothly, maybe too smoothly in fact. Maybe this was going to be fine. I waved to my two siblings waiting outside the airport hall and proceeded to the gate.

The immigration officer demanded for my passport and asked where I was travelling to. I told him South Africa. He looked at me and asked if I lived in South Africa or just visiting. I chose the latter. Unknown to me, if you are travelling on a new passport, 'virgin passports', which means you do not have any evidence of previous travels in the passport, you are an automatic target for the officers.

He asked me to move aside while another officer ushered me into some dark room. Even though it was my first time going through immigration, I knew something was wrong. I became even more anxious. My mind was racing. I immediately remembered the bogus traveller's cheque that I had arranged earlier because I did not have enough travel allowance with me. I only had $350 on me. That was all I could manage to raise. A friend had promised me additional $100 but he was running late, and I had to leave for the airport. He called when I was already on my way to say he was at my house to drop the money. I thanked him and told him not to worry any longer as I was already on my way to the airport. He apologized profusely blaming the traffic. He had to jump out of his car to get on a commercial motorbike called 'okada' when he realized he might not make it to me on time. He still wanted to drop the money regardless and asked if he could drop it with my sister. I thanked him greatly. It was a true show of kindness on his part. Not many will still go ahead considering the intended beneficiary was no longer available. Indeed, the money would still be quite useful. I used it to settle part of the loan I had taken from my sister as part of the trip.

Unjani Mfwethu?

What I had thought to be a wise contingency plan was now my nemesis. There were two other officers waiting in the room. They were asking numerous questions while searching through my hand luggage and pockets. They wanted to know everything possible - my details, what I did for a living, why I was travelling and how much I had with me etc. They asked to see my bag and went through my documents. I had to part with $50 as an appeasement for the problematic traveller's cheque. They stamped me out. What mattered most was that I was free to go to the boarding gate. I immediately called my girlfriend and narrated my ordeal. She was just glad it all went well, and I was on my way out of the country.

I looked outside the SAA Boeing 747 to the surrounds of the Murtala Muhammed International Airport. My thoughts getting more sombre as I watched the aircraft begin its slow taxi to the runway. This was it! I made a few calls to my girlfriend and mum, sent out a few more SMS messages before finally switching off my phone. I closed my eyes and said a few prayers before take-off. Nothing could have prepared me for the unsettling feeling of the aircraft pulling away from the ground. Not wanting to disclose my panic and first timer status to nearby passengers, I held on tight to my seat and hoped to God that I survive the flight.

Leaving one's family and country of birth is never easy, especially for economic reasons. There are always many counter arguments against leaving. Despite the years and months of preparations, one is never shielded from the sudden waves of self-doubts that come in the final moment: is this the right decision? Will it work out and will it be worth it? It can truly be overwhelming. It was a very lonely journey, but one that I was looking forward to.

At the time of boarding the plane in Lagos, I was still not convinced on the plan. I had a short-term visa and wanted to go and explore. I decided to go with an open mind, nevertheless. Yety had suggested that I pack all my essentials just in case I changed my mind and decided to stay back. She knows from experience how difficult it can be settling in a new country and how scant money can be. I am glad that I listened. It would eventually take me about a year to be able to afford new clothes. I remember another friend, Abdul, who told me how lucky I was to have brought along some clothes when leaving home. He had a more difficult experience. His brother, who invited him over, had told him not to bother. He convinced him that South Africa was like Europe. There are big malls all over and you will not have any problems getting great stuff. However, what he omitted to tell was that those great stuff do not come free, you must pay for them. It reminded me of the joke my brother –in –law (in the States) made as soon as I arrived in South Africa. He asked if I had been to the malls and if it did not feel like I should buy everything on display.

Dominique insisted that I had to purchase some essentials: a phone, winter jacket, a pair of comfortable shoes and of course my visa extension. A quick mental math told me that I was already in 'red'. The visa extension alone would cost R500 and had to be done within the next 30 days. I added a R20 world call card to the list. I had to call home.

For the first time since leaving Nigeria, it was starting to feel like I was settling in. Dominique had hooked me up with a job where he was working – alongside another Nigerian friend, Ola. I could start earning some money immediately. Dominique had reminded me of how important it was to sort out my visas. There was no time to waste but of course, money was important. I had come to realize quickly – maybe too quickly – how elusive the South African Rand was. All around me, it just seemed like a mission impossible to save as little as R100. I was told stories of many migrants, including friends of ours, who were unable to renew their papers simply because of their inabilities to put together the R500 fees. They were living 'illegally' for months and years and had to live in the shadows, while ducking and diving from police everywhere. It was not a pleasant story. I started to ponder at very early on how to navigate this reality.

The 90's were particularly very turbulent times in Nigeria, politically and economically. The country was inundated with incessant military coups and military dictators. The economy was in shambles due to a sustained period of poor leadership and unfettered corruption. Unemployment was at record highs and university staff members were in and out of strikes. Tertiary institutions were on the brink of collapse, as was the case with other levels of education. There was a widespread of hopelessness in the society.

I graduated at the University of Lagos with high hopes for a well-paying job. Like many graduates at the time, hopes were easily dashed, and dreams shattered. After 5 years of fruitless search for a decent job, life was becoming very bleak and I was increasingly looking more morose and melancholier. Even as the economy started to open a little better due to the privatization efforts of the new, returning president, Olusegun Obasanjo, getting into the mainstream employment sector became more difficult the longer one stayed unemployed. It was a catch 22 situation. Employers demanded previous relevant experience before one could be considered. I was a little too proud to consider some of the alternatives which included but not limited to, seeking favours from friends of families or politically connected persons. For some reason, I just did not want to owe that much a favour to anyone. I would tell my friends and family repeatedly that I know I will get there. I just needed to believe and stay focused on God.

It was not a difficult choice to make. I was aware of the prospects of venturing out of the country in pursuit of greener pastures. I had many friends who had regularly went to the UK and the US for 'holiday jobs' during school breaks and would return with loads of foreign currency to the chagrin of many of us on campus. Their exploits could be seen in the parade of 'tokunbo' (imported) cars on campus as well as the designer clothes. Every young Nigerian at the time, perhaps even worse now, shared the dream of such exploits. Later, stories of friends and cousins who had relocated overseas would make the yearning grow stronger. So, it was a no brainer that when things became extra tough, I started to consider leaving the country as a matter of urgency. I repeatedly told myself and my girlfriend that if only I could leave the country, things would fall into place. It was a belief born out of a strong hope as well as naïve confidence in stories heard.

'Travelling out' as it was called, was an industry in itself. There were all sorts of players involved in the business of 'travelling out' and as to be expected, stories of fraudulent practices and travel scams were prevalent. We even heard of many travellers who had become stranded midway to their destinations and having to engage in all manner of practices to survive and to continue their journey. Nevertheless, the success stories of friends, family and even strangers often eclipsed the dangers recounted. Everyone felt strongly that his or her own story will be a successful one. What were the options anyway? I began to intensify efforts to leave the country as the situation become even more deplorable. Securing the required funds was the hardest part but as the cliché goes, 'where there is a will there is a way'. I managed to pull the necessary resources together with the help of family and friends.

It was now time for divine intervention.

I attended Redeem Church in Lagos at the time. During a special prayer week sometime in January 2002, the pastor stood up and asked the congregation to ask God for a special request. It had to be a request that mattered the most to us. To make it even more special, we needed to sacrifice the one

Unjani Mfwethu?

thing that was special to us in exchange for this request from God. I knew what my request was, and I also knew what it was that I was willing to give up in exchange. I did as demanded in faith. Shortly after, in February, I received a call from the South African Embassy notifying me that my visa application was approved. I was elated! I had a few other visa applications to other countries pending but I remembered vividly as the Pastor, during the service, had warned the congregation to watch out for the first breakthrough - that would be the sign. I knew then that I would have to go with South Africa, even though it was the least known to me and many.

South Africa at the time was not the destination of choice for many in my country compared to the United Kingdom, Canada, or the States. Not that South Africa was not popular among Nigerians, we knew South Africa for its much-televised struggle against White oppressive rule, Apartheid, including Sarafina. South African music was also much loved in Nigeria. I remember as kids singing and dancing to Brenda Fassie, Yvonne Chaka Chaka, Mariam Makeba, Hugh Masekela, and a host of others. It was just not one that we saw as a place of economic refuge back in the 90's and early 2000's (This would come to change as the years went by). I did envisage myself visiting one day as a student of international law and politics. It happened sooner than expected.

I was not disappointed at all. At least from the optics. Besides the world class infrastructure, I interacted with highly sophisticated people across racial divides. Black South Africans were particularly interesting to me. Their natural affiliation to everything local – the creativity, music, and language – was completely different to where I was coming from. We leaned heavily towards things foreign and considered our native languages 'vernacular'. I heard music everywhere I turned. You were not considered 'on the edge' to be seen dancing on the streets. Men and women alike all paid great attention to their hair. Young black professionals, male and female, in traffic would engage hawkers and street kids without any form of discrimination. It did not seem to matter what side of the social ladder you belonged to. The average person was very accessible. Little wonder the seat of government, the Union building, is in the heart of the city with no heavy security presence, as is the case in other countries. I was observing and ingesting a lot about this new country and very fast too.

While it was refreshing to take in all that was happening around me, I needed to face a more compelling reality. Dominique's flatmates and landlady were not happy that he brought in another guest to an already crowded flat. He had lied, albeit unsuccessfully, to them that I was only visiting for few days and will be out in no time. We were under immense pressure to find a new accommodation, it seemed like there is never a dull moment in a migrant's life. Dominique was not as troubled as I was. He told me that it was a blessing in disguise. He never really liked Sunnyside and had been planning on leaving anyway.

He immediately contacted his network of fellow migrants and in no time, we were introduced to Serikit, the German lady. She was desperate to find a tenant and for some odd reason, took a liking to me. She named me 'babyface' on the spot and wanted to know when we would be moving in. Everything was so fast. We arranged the required deposit and one month rent in advance, pro rata, which amounted to a total of R1300. I was already in deficit less than a month in the country, but I was still in high spirits. God will make a way I repeated to myself.

Moving to Walker Street was a wise decision. It was a lot quieter and a more upmarket part of Sunnyside. It is midway between Brooklyn and Sunnyside and more appropriate for work purposes - at least for me. Dominique had to walk a little longer to the west. While Sunnyside was predominantly black, you could still find a few middle-class white families in the neighbourhood. It felt like a proper apartment! The pay phone booth right in front of the building was the icing on the cake for me at the time.

This phone booth would later become a contentious matter between Dominique and me. He could not understand why I would spend R50 on a calling card per month or sometimes twice a month to call my family and friends, when we could perhaps use the money to add to the monthly groceries. He did not have such commitments and so could not understand. I was too strong willed to be influenced otherwise. I stood my ground and continued without fail to make calls home. Eventually Dominique and other friends also started to call home more regularly. I remember accompanying a friend to call his mum and I could hear the mum admonishing him for not calling more frequently and the desperate attempt by my friend to explain how difficult things were and how expensive it was to call from South Africa. He was telling the truth.

Hawking is not the easiest task for anyone, not the least for foreigners. We had to contend with several challenges ranging from language barriers to all sorts of stereotypes including, 'all Nigerians must have drugs in their possession'. The relatively high crime in the country did not also help matters. There were indeed many hazards to the job.

Unjani Mfwethu?

Trespassing, which is hawking, poses the greatest danger to our trade. We have been confronted with business owners brandishing guns in our faces and demanding we exit their premises. I remember working in a territory with Ola and Dominique in an isolated area of Silver Lakes, Pretoria. We had been working the small business area for a while with no success. Many of the businesses would not let us into the premises. The scorching heat on that afternoon did not help matters, we were all looking exhausted.

Suddenly, we saw a car drive out of a Battery testing center and the electric gate still opened. Without thinking, I attempted to slide in quickly with my two friends in tow. I had barely taken more than three steps when I saw the most scary and angriest dog I had ever seen in my life, barging towards the gate -towards us. I was transfixed and did not notice my friends sprinting across the road leaving me to my fate - everything seemed to be in slow motion. It felt like the menacing dog had hypnotized me. I stood there waiting to be mauled. But it was not to be. God came through again. The electric gate slammed shut just as the dog approached. All I heard was a loud bang on the gate. I locked eyes with the dog still pretty shaken up! In that instant, the business owner came out of her office and shouted at me to 'voetsek'! I regained my mind and ran to my friends across the road, whom by now were giggling and teasing me about the incident. We all agreed to exit Silver Lakes immediately. It was time to go to a friendly site. Dominique needed to pick up some money from Sarah in Pretoria West.

Sarah was a very warm and beautiful woman from Mabopane Township in Pretoria. She worked in a document dispatch company in the industrial part of Pretoria West. I could sense her warmth the very day Dominique introduced me to her. She had all the attributes of a caring mother. Dominique had told us how she had been God sent. He made more money through her help in less than six months than anything he had made during the past 3 years. Sarah loved African fabrics and had nudged Dominique to venture into the business early on. They had met when Dominique had walked into the warehouse in Pretoria West to sell perfumes. The ladies on the floor had quickly introduced him to their floor manager, Sarah. In her typical nature, she warmed up to Dominique and eventually encouraged the other workers to also order some perfumes. It was the reason that Dominique stuck to that territory for as long as were in Pretoria. It was not just a source of steady flow of income, but also a place of remarkable hospitality.

The rest of us, in no time, were also welcomed into Sarah's open arms. She invited us regularly to her home where we met her equally awesome family and her police officer boyfriend. They all were very protective of us – their Nigeria brothers. The police officer boyfriend would, on one occasion in the township, come to our defence when a handful of the township boys were 'unhappy' with our presence in their neighbourhood, cursing that no 'amakwerekwere', a derogatory term reserved for African migrants, was allowed in the township. It was the first time I heard the word. Sarah's daughter had scolded the boys and immediately asked that we cut short the stroll and return to their house. She recounted the ugly experience to her mum and her mum's boyfriend and he immediately got up and asked to be taken to the scene. Such was the extent of the hospitality we enjoyed from Sarah's family. It was the first time I felt at home in South Africa.

Each time we walked past policemen on our way to the office or to sell, I was always reminded of the urgency to extend my permit. The Sunnyside police particularly were notorious for stopping everyone who looked 'African ex SA' at random and demanding their permits. It was the story of many African and Asian migrants. My friends would always tell of many 'close shaves' moments. For instance, in Sunnyside on a Sunday afternoon, when many migrants were hanging around the Sunny Park mall and surrounds, suddenly immigration officials and police descended on the area and begun to apprehend foreigners - lining them up to be picked up by standby vans.

Two of my friends were among those apprehended on that day. I still remember the deep fear in their eyes as they recounted the ordeal. They arrived in South Africa on the same day from Nigeria and only had a week left on their visas on arrival. With very little opportunity to earn a decent living, it was difficult to raise the required funds to either extend their visas or seek alternative means. They immediately became illegal immigrants, shortly on arrival- a status that would last for more than a year. It was exactly a year and three months when they were picked up in Sunnyside.

It was a long line of migrants whose documents needed to be verified at the immigration office. My friends had one thought in mind - they could not go back home now and in this manner. A moment of distraction on the part of the officers was all that was required. The two friends made a run for it, running desperately into the corners and dark alleys of Sunnyside with one of the officers in pursuit. It was difficult to keep up with any of the two. The friends split up and quickly disappeared into the corners. It took two days for the friends to be reunited again. They had to keep a low profile for fear of being picked up through intelligence. It was not a way to live. I knew I had to act fast.

It was one thing to have the resolve but another to have the funds. Having exhausted the meagre sum of money that I brought with me to the country, I was now in deficit from the bills for the new accommodation. The visa agent that we got advised that the total cost would be about R750, including the official application fee of R500 plus R250 agent fee. That was just a lot of money. I had no idea where to begin. Every day when I looked at my passport (we were obliged to carry our passports with us. Many migrants face an additional burden when their passports are misplaced or stolen), I was reminded of the urgency of the situation. It was mindboggling.

I thought of reaching out to family for support but did not want to send a wrong signal so early on. I kept thinking of alternatives. I thought of asking Mark for a loan, except I had only started working for him. Every passing day without an assurance was a heartache. Suddenly, all the struggles of back home seemed like child's play compared to what might be if I became 'stuck' in this new country. I had to figure something out. Everyone in my circle had no means and those outside did not care so much. It was a very hard realization that so little could make such a big difference in one's fate. The more I ranted about my dilemma, the more frustrated some were. They thought I was just being unnecessarily righteous.

Not feeling like watching any movies, I accompanied Dominique to the UNISA campus in Mucklenuek. He was a registered student at the university and promised that he could get me into the IT lab where I could read and send emails. It sounded like a great idea. The commercial internet cafes in Sunnyside were quite expensive. A mere 15 minutes would set one back about R50 – half of the time still trying to download your mails. UNISA seemed to be a lifesaver. With surprising ease, I managed to get into the IT lab as promised.

I had many unread mails from my siblings, friends, and some of the universities I had been applying to in the UK and Canada. There was another email from a friend from my university days whom I did not realise was in South Africa. He said he was told by another friend that I was now in SA. He had been in South Africa since we graduated 5 years ago. He worked for an engineering company in the North West but had a sister in Pretoria. He wanted me to call him. I was quite excited to read from him. He was one of the very good and funny guys on campus. He was also into student politics. I wanted desperately to see a familiar face that was really settled into the system. I am sure he could give me valuable tips.

Dominique and I left the lab just before nightfall. I never liked walking at night at all. There were just so many things that could wrong. Ola had been mugged recently on his way back to his apartment at night. He knew something bad was about to happen the moment he saw them walking towards him. It was too late to make a run for it. They held a knife to his side and demanded that he hand over his phone and wallet. The incident had left him very upset and the rest of us a little more careful – well maybe not Dominique, he always felt invincible.

Somewhere on the corner of Troy and Rissik Street, we saw a parked police car. Dominique immediately asked that we cross to the other side of the road, but in the same instant, two officers came out of the car, and immediately gestured to us to come over. They asked who we were, where we are from, and as usual, our identification papers. Thankfully, I had my passport on me and handed it over to them with my visa page. They asked for Dominique's, who continued to search frantically for his UNISA student ID in his wallet. After a few minutes of no success, they asked both of us to get into the van. They drove us to our apartment and followed us up to the door for Dominique to retrieve his ID. I suspect the real reason was to confirm our residence and to possibly look around for any suspicious activities. It was a huge relief that Serikit and Thabo were not in the apartment when the police accompanied us. We would not have heard the last of it. I thought to myself how different the evening could have turned out to be had my visa expired. It was a taste of what my fellow migrant brothers and sisters go through daily.

A week after I received my friend's email, we were going to meet up by Shoprite on Esselen street cnr Celiers. He had told me that he would be coming to Pretoria to see his sister and that we should meet up. I saw a white Jetta park close to me and noticed his big smile beaming through the driver's window. I was quite delighted to see him. He parked and gestured to one of the 'parking assistants' on the street to keep watch over his car. We hugged and quickly brought each other up to speed. I was happy to hear about his journey. Even though he had a sister who was doing well in the country (she and her husband had a medical practice in Pretoria) when he arrived, it was still not an easy ride. He sympathized with me and gave several tips including to make sure I register for my post graduate degree as soon as possible. SA, he said, 'lacked skilled labour but has abundant unskilled labour', so I needed to make the transition as quickly as possible. Time flies when you are having fun they say. My friend had to leave and would only be back again in Pretoria in about a month. He promised to always check on me and said that he was only a phone call away if I needed anything.

We shook hands and I felt him squeeze some notes in my hand almost embarrassingly. He apologized that it was little, but he was sure that it would help. I was quite surprised. Even though the thought had crossed my mind to ask him for some help regarding my papers, I was unable to bring myself to it. The conversation had gone on and on beautifully that I did not want to spoil the moment with such requests as desperate as I was. I waved him on, and quickly checked the notes. I was completely taken aback! I counted ten R50 notes. Oh, my word! R500 bucks! I just stood in the middle of the road looking into the abyss! For a moment forgetting that I could be robbed standing by the robot! I broke into a short run, made my way to a nearby garage to catch my breath. I pulled out my phone and called him immediately. I could not stop rambling. All he said was that he wished me all the best.

Dominique and I arranged to meet the agent at the Cullinan home affairs office to file my visa extension application.

I only had few days left on my validity. The agent had advised that filing at Cullinan was much quicker and less cumbersome compared to Pretoria. I liked the serenity of the town. I thought perhaps someday I could move to Cullinan. The filing was quicker than expected. All the required documents were submitted, and the required fee paid. We were given an application receipt which also serves as a temporary permit pending the finalization of my application. I had been assured by the agent that visa extensions were routine and rarely ever denied. I had nothing to worry about. I had applied for a six-month visa extension, although we were told that you could only apply for the same duration as initially given, in my case three months but I thought to try anyway.

I was happy to leave with my temporary permit and thankful to God and my friend for the timely miracle. I had just narrowly escaped and could now focus on unwrapping the beauty that South Africa has in stock. I still refused to eat 'pap', one of the most popular South African staple foods, even as my friends warned that I would have no choice but to eat it, when real hunger grips me. I guess I would just have to ensure so that it does not happen. Time to step up the game.

Unjani Mfwethu?

CHAPTER 3
Unmasking the Country

Time seems to move faster than usual for migrants. Even though I had only been in the country for six months, it felt like I had been around for eternity. Work had taken me into the deep corners of the city and the hearts of its people, and contrary to my initial impression when I just arrived; I now started to observe in more detail the socio-economic conditions of the country. Even though in some very notable ways, South Africa was a far cry from Nigeria and competes strongly with the Western world but, the high level of poverty, crime, increasing informal economy, and dilapidating infrastructure in certain areas in the townships reminded me so much of the country I left behind.

These contradictions would ignite in me, a strong desire to know more about the history of the people of South Africa. Every day as I go about selling to all manner of people, I would make mental notes on discussions around culture, politics, and economic life of the average South African. It was a fascinating observation and for the first time in my life, the phenomenon of race, segregation, and economic inequality (as a consequence of racial divide), would start to resonate with me beyond my political science classes at university.

By this time, I had decided to give South Africa a chance. I was impressed by the infrastructure, the people and more importantly, I kept in mind the encounter in church prior to my leaving Nigeria. I told my family that I had decided to stay and give it a try. Given that I had now secured a temporary relief with my permit, I needed to explore the prospect of studying for a postgraduate degree.

However, I had noticed that my academic interest was starting to shift from political economy and international relations to marketing and business. I guess the newly acquired skill picked up on the streets, selling perfumes was largely responsible for the new shift. I discussed with a few people in my circle - including Mark and Tshepo (who were very supportive of the idea) and decided to go to the UNISA campus to make inquiries about registering for a postgraduate program in Marketing Management. I picked up the brochure from the Learner Support Officer who asked if I had a South African Matric Certificate - I would have thought that a bachelor's degree would be a more important prerequisite. In any case, we concluded that my GCE O' Level certificate would suffice for a Matric exemption and thus, I could be cleared to enrol for the postgraduate program. I would have to request for my undergraduate transcripts from the University of Lagos to be mailed directly to UNISA (I made a note to mail a copy to myself - it would come to matter greatly in later years), submit an application, pay the required fees and yes, provide a study permit. Dominique advised that the provisional admission letter from the University could be used to apply for the study permit at the Department of Home Affairs. I would again need another medical report, and thankfully, my previous police report was still valid.

Sometime in August 2002, Mark told us that we were all invited to the annual Sales Meeting of the company in Johannesburg. All the regional sales representatives and business owners would be present. The Pretoria team had grown in size. Besides Ola, Dominique, and I, we now had a Congolese guy with a PhD in Law, as well as a black South African lady working with us. Mark had asked that we all meet up at the head office for the meeting.

Dominique and I decided to travel by train. I was looking forward to it as it would be my first time on a train in South Africa. We almost missed the train - that's classic Dominique and found ourselves rushing through the gates to catch the train. I looked around for a suitable seat while trying to catch my breath. The coach we were in, seemed too 'glamorous' to me. I immediately asked Dominique if he was sure we were in the right coach. It just looked like a first-class coach to me. My friend put on a wicked grin and asked if I thought this was Nigeria. He said arrogantly that these are all standard coaches and made a joke that he is glad that I left Nigeria. Instinctively, I asked about the ticket and he mumbled that he had us covered with a student pass. It was not the first time he tried to show off with his many UNISA student benefits.

I settled down to enjoy the train ride, taking in every bit of the scenery as the train made its journey towards Johannesburg. Dominque was quick to mention that the coaches' got super packed during rush hours and so he wanted us to be out of Johannesburg just after lunch time. I muttered that all would depend on how the meeting goes. With that, he brought out the previous day's papers - I still have not gotten over the size of South Africa's daily newspapers. I always joked with friends that one needed four hands to manoeuvre it.

A sudden movement jolted me out of my thoughts. I looked up to see two ticket officers - I noticed one had a set of handcuffs with him - looking down at me and asking for our tickets. I immediately tapped Dominique and mentioned that there were officers demanding our tickets. Without looking up, he said that I should not worry, that they were just playing with us. It did not look that way to me. The officers lost their patience and barked out louder for the tickets. Now they had his attention. He started to search his pockets frantically – I waited for him to produce his student card, but nothing came out. The officers immediately unlocked the handcuffs and demanded that we produce the tickets, pay a fine or be arrested. I was confused. What happened to the student card? Dominique then looked at me and asked if I had any money on me. I was stunned but even more stunned when I realized that the fine was ten times the cost of an ordinary ticket. I paid R50 for the fine. This was the money I had been saving for weeks to buy a World Call Card. I had plans to call my family the coming weekend. I was livid!

We did not speak for the remainder of the journey. I narrated the ordeal to Ola once we were reunited at the meeting venue. He laughed so hard and said he was not surprised at all. Everyone knew Dominique for his many antics and carelessness. He warned me to just be more careful around him, so he does not get me into trouble with his foolish ways. I did not know which was more painful – the idea of almost being arrested for such a stupid act or the loss of my R50.

Either way, I was very upset with him.

I was greatly impressed by the presentations given during the Sales Reps meeting at the head office in Johannesburg. I listened attentively as the regional heads, franchisees, reported on their income figures. While it was gratifying to watch as the top achieving sales representatives received their awards, my mind was fixated on the business owners. They seem to be making the most money next to the business founders themselves. I started to dissect the business model. It was not difficult to buy a 'franchise' and set up your own team, I heard during the presentation. The company was even willing to provide some support, provided one puts up the initial capital for inventory and can demonstrate an existing team of two at the minimum. The company will provide a tester kit for free. A new idea was birthed in my mind on that day.

Beaming with so many ideas, I made my way to McDonalds in Acadia on a lovely Sunday evening to meet with Ola and Dominique. I could tell that spring was approaching. I had barely survived my first winter in the country and was eagerly waiting for the break of spring (which was still some days away), but it felt good not to have to layer up so much again. I watched as students went up and down the street and hoped that the guys were early. I had bought us tickets for a movie later that evening. We also needed to discuss all the ideas in my head in more detail. I had hinted Dominique on the matter, and it seemed I already had his buy-in. He is a rebel by nature and relishes any opportunity to rock the boat. Ola on the other hand was more of a stability guy.

Once again, the easiest part, it appeared, was getting the team - Dominique and Ola - to go along with me (I tried, however unsuccessfully, to enlist other friends who had not been a part of the business in the past. They were eventually useful to us in other ways later in the business), raising the necessary start-up capital however proved to be harder than I thought.

We could only come up with about R800 among the three of us. Our business plan required a minimum of R5000 to kick start the business. This would cover the inventory cost of about R2000 (40 bottles at R50 per bottle), transport and living costs, at least for the first month or two. We had to be conservative in our revenue projections even if we had an existing client base. It was obvious that we needed to look for external support if our dream of breaking free and owning our own business was going to be realized. I started to run through my network - not that there were a lot of people that

I knew who could provide me with some loan in such a short notice. I told myself I could probably only approach three or four people. Two of the four quickly declined. I reached out to my brother-in-law and Yety, and between the two, I was able to raise R3000. Dominque also managed to raise additional R4000 from his brother in the UK. We were off to a very good start. We were super motivated and ready to move. But first, we needed to engage with Mark to inform him of our plans and thank him for his great support. We did not think he would be displeased, given that his team had grown significantly, and we had been instrumental in helping train the new recruits.

We congregated in Mark's permanent hotel room on a Friday after the day's delivery. We chose that day specifically because we knew he would be in a very good mood given that we had a good number of deliveries for the day. We were right! The day went as planned and the overall team's hit rate was over 95%. Mark wanted the team to stay back for drinks. It was a good time to strike. We told Mark during drinks that we would like to have a private meeting with him later that evening if he did not mind. He was curious and wondered what it was. But we insisted on having the meeting just among us four. After drinks, we all said goodbye to the others and the four of us left in Mark's old Jetta to his hotel. It turned out we were completely wrong in our expectation. Mark was furious! He jumped out of his seat and became very animated - we had always worried about his temper. We looked at each other in hidden panic. Mark lamented that we were a bunch of ingrates while staring hard at me. He told us in unequivocal terms that there was no way we could break free and hope to still be with the company. No one would give us stock. He would make sure of that! He started to smoke unstoppably and told us to get out of his room calling us all sorts of names.

Phew! We did not see that coming. I had imagined a bit of disappointment, but not the total hostility and rage he displayed. We had to think fast about how to proceed. Obviously, we could not go back to him given the way the relationship turned. We suddenly found ourselves 'out of a job' while not even off the ground with our entrepreneurial journey. If we are kicked out of the company and could not get stock, that without doubt was the end of our dream.

The team agreed that we had to go to the head office to meet the owners of the business and present our case. We had not come that far in our plans to be defeated by one man's greed and outbursts. We would meet the duo of Peter and Chris and hoped that they would see an opportunity to grow their business even further. We would show take them our plans, our existing joint client base, and our combined numbers - historic and projected. We reasoned that these are businessmen and the only thing that should matter is a business rationale. Chris and Peter are South Africa Jews in their mid-40s. Chris was the technical brain behind the company. He is a chemical engineer by training while Peter, is the business mind. Peter has a great personality and gives the impression that you could always talk to him. We knew that if we got through to Peter, we would be fine.

It would turn out that the duo was already aware of our 'great mutiny'. They welcomed us warmly as we arrived in their office, and immediately asked us what was going on in Pretoria. As expected, Peter seemed a lot more enthusiastic as we narrated our story. Chris, as we were to later find out, was more concerned about the feasibility of our plan. How do we plan to pay for the inventory, and can we be trusted with his intellectual property?

After a very long meeting, Chris and Peter seemed to be coming around. They agreed in principle that we had a good plan, and they were quite impressed with our audacity. There were happy to retain us within the business and provide necessary support, but on some conditions though.

Unjani Mfwethu?

They told us we would have to trade outside Gauteng. They would not allow cannibalization within the company. Mark already had Pretoria, Johannesburg and surrounds belonged to another. Western Cape, Free State, and Durban in Kwa-Zulu Natal were also taken. That left us with Mpumalanga, Eastern Cape, and the Northern Cape. Furthermore, they required full upfront payment of all stocks including packaging and delivery cost. We agreed to the latter terms and advised that we would have to deliberate on the issue of territories. We honestly had not given much thought to the idea of trading outside of Gauteng. We had hoped that even if we had to leave Pretoria for Mark, maybe Johannesburg would accommodate us given its size. We therefore needed more time to think about our next move. Before we departed, Chris and Peter called Mark and provided a summary of the days meeting. Mark insisted that we keep away from his territory, his clients, his team and that we surrender his tester kits, order books - including all pending orders. I thought of my precious recurring order for Tshepo. It was a small price to pay but I had to stay far away from him!

South Africa is a relatively big country in terms of landmass. It comprises of nine provinces. Each distinctly different from the other. It is a stunningly beautiful country to travel and explore. But in 2002, we knew very little of the country. Of all three of us, only Dominique had been outside Gauteng. He had visited Cape Town in the Western Cape and Bloemfontein in the Free State. The gravity of our plan started to dawn on us. How can we make this work? Which city do we choose and what will be the criteria? We thought about each of the open territories. What did we know about these places, do we know anyone there? Are there significant black population that we could count on to support us? It was a very tasking exercise in market mapping and market development.

As we continued to deliberate on which territories to shortlist, it was obvious that we had little or no intel on all the listed open territories. Everyone we knew only knew people in Cape Town, Durban, or Bloemfontein. We were playing around with two options at the time: stay in Pretoria but travel to the designated territory to sell aggressively for a week and then return on delivery days. The second option was to pack up and relocate fully to a new territory. The latter option seemed more practical and cost efficient. But the question remained, where do we go?

I suddenly remembered that a friend back home had mentioned in one of the emails I received early on as I arrived in South Africa, that a close friend of his was based in South

Unjani Mfwethu?

Africa. He even told me that I would recognize him when we meet. He said he was a classmate of my sister. I had not given much thought to the email at the time, but in the quest to search through my entire network in the country, I went back to the email and realized that the friend stays in Nelspruit, Mpumalanga. I went back to my email, retrieved his friend's contact number, and managed to get him on phone. It turned out that he knew me quite well - seen me on many occasions when I would visit my sister in class, as well as on their graduation ceremony - and was glad that we reconnected. He told me he relocated to South Africa immediately after graduation with the hope of making it further to the UK. He said he was told by his travel agent in Nigeria, that it was easier to obtain travel visa from South Africa to the UK. He had been in SA for about 3 years and no prospect of leaving the country after many visa refusals. He left Johannesburg for Nelspruit to work as a high school teacher in one of the private schools in the province.

Chris and Peter were thrilled that we finally decided. They thought Nelspruit was a promising territory. They have long had their eyes on the city, and they felt no team was more deserving of such a virgin territory. They were confident that we would succeed. We shook hands and formally entered into a business agreement. It was the beginning of a new chapter in our lives, in my life. I again remembered my encounter at the church prior to my departure for South Africa. I remained positive. Later that evening, I made two calls to my investors and provided a detailed update. All they cared about was that the business would be successful and that I would find fulfilment. They wished me well.

Before departing for Nelspruit, I decided to attend to my growing locks. Ola had advised that I go to the salon to have a professional tidy it up just as he had done. A few of our friends worked as barbers at a salon in the CBD, so it was not hard to get one of the ladies to agree to fixing my hair. I screamed as the lady held the first strand of hair to weave into locks. I could not have imagined the pain involved! The ladies were having so much fun watching me twist and groan in pain with each weave. I suspect that she was doing it on purpose - pulling so hard at my skull, just so that I can appreciate what women go through.

On the 30th of September, in the full glare of Spring, all three of us embarked on a four-hour long bus ride to Nelspruit, where we would transfer to another bus for a two-hour ride to Kabokweni. Leaving Pretoria, my first city of abode in South Africa, that morning was emotional. We had said farewell to friends the day before and promised to always come back whenever possible. Serikit had cried in her

Unjani Mfwethu?

characteristic manner and gave me a bear hug, while waving Dominique on. She said she had loved living with us and that she would miss us so much. That much was true. I thanked her also for her hospitality and told her to say a big hello to Thabo. She said we were welcome to come over whenever we were back in town.

We spent almost a year in Nelspruit. It was a completely different city to Pretoria. Nelspruit was a growing city with fewer than three shopping malls. While Pretoria was a mix of all businesses, Nelspruit was largely dominated by small sized professional services company and government departments. What Nelspruit, or the region, lacked in terms of size and business territory, it made up for in terms of the depth or richness of experience it provided. Living in Kabokweni for the entire time we were in the region, allowed us to be deeply immersed in the distinct township experience of South Africa. One that would change my perception of the country and its history forever.

We arrived late in Kabokweni. My friend, Larry, had been waiting a while for us at the bus park. It had been a tiring journey, but the beautiful scenery- eye popping hills and mountains - made it a lot more bearable. Kabokweni was different to the township I had visited in Pretoria, Mabopane.

The township reminded me of smaller towns in Nigeria. The ambience was very African. The bus park, the hawkers and surprisingly too, I spotted what looked like cassava Tubers being sold at the bus park. For the first time arriving in SA, it felt like I was in Africa. Larry could see the reaction in my eyes. Ola and Dominque had the same reaction as well. He misinterpreted our reaction to be that of disappointment and immediately tried to give some explanations or apology. I quickly told him to stop. I reminded him that he had warned me earlier before embarking on the journey. It was our decision to come and we are very grateful for his hospitality. I reassured him that we were prepared to make it work whatever it took.

We were surprised to find that Kabokweni was home to many other Nigerians and other African foreigners in fact. Most were employed as teachers in the privately run high schools in the region that catered for middle class to rich kids from neighbouring countries. The schools were predominantly boarding schools. Apparently, these private schools were able to employee foreign teachers without having to adhere to the strict requirements expected of South African public schools.

Most of the foreign teachers, even though they were not professional teachers, they were highly educated professionals. Some with postgraduate degrees from their countries of origin. It was a win- win situation for all.

The weekend we arrived in Kabokweni, Larry made sure that we were adequately introduced to the community. We met his neighbours, South African locals, and other Nigerians in the community. The meetings were very helpful in preparing for our 'attack' on the city of Nelspruit that following Monday. We needed help with the logistics and found enough assistance from the people we spoke to. We knew that we could create a strategy on how to approach the territory and how to divide among ourselves once we completed the initial sight-survey the coming Monday.

The daily commute from Kabokweni to Nelspruit and back was exhausting. It did not cross our mind to move to the city as we were having so much fun living in the township. We were amid family. The Nigerian community provided a crucial social support and the South African locals who were our neighbours ensured that we felt at home and safe. We felt at ease at the local pubs, called shebeens. We managed to sell a few perfumes on the local buses to fellow passengers whom in the short time spent, had become well known to one another.

We truly felt at home. Not even an ugly incident at Larry's place with fellow Nigerians and some locals, could make us leave the township. It was a day like no other. We were unaware that Larry had been involved in a brawl with a fellow Nigerian over a television set. According to him, he had sold the TV to a Nigerian brother who was also his colleague, with the understanding that he, the buyer, would pay a deposit, and thereafter pay the balance at the next pay day. For some reason, our brother did not honour his part of the agreement come pay day. Larry was furious and went to retrieve his TV set forcefully. The Nigerian brother felt cheated and he interpreted Larry's actions as intimidation, perhaps backed by his three guests – Ola, Dominque and myself. In a surprising move, our Nigerian brother colluded with some South African locals to avenge what he termed an assault on him. On the day of the attack, we were relaxing in the room. Suddenly, the door burst open and the next thing we saw were strange people pointing guns at us. In the same moment, our Nigerian brother stormed in with another South African guy whom I recognized as one of my perfume clients. They immediately picked up the TV set and threatened to shoot if we made any move. I was shocked and scared stiff at the same time. I had never had a gun pointed at me before. I asked the South African guy that I recognized, why they were doing this, and he told me to shut up and to ask my brother. They were gone as quickly as they appeared. Our neighbours who had seen everything, called the police, but we decided not to open a case on the advice of the Nigerian community. They told us that they would be handling the matter as a community.

Unbeknownst to us at the time, we were leaving the city life of Pretoria for a more communal lifestyle in Kabokweni, where everyone was each other's keeper. All the migrant communities lived in peace with the host community. Even though it was not our most comfortable living, it was by far our richest in terms of experience. We became involved in the affairs of the Nigerian community in the township. In all, there must have been about a 100 Nigerians living there during the time.

I remember when one of the members of the Nigerian community was arrested and detained at the Nelspruit Police Station. The elders of the community had tasked us to go to the station to secure his release. The detainee's wife could not accompany us as she did not have valid permits at the time. It was very heart-breaking to see her and her two little kids in a state of fear and not knowing what would happen to her husband and their dad. Thankfully, we were able to resolve the matter and return him safely to the hands of his loved ones.

While our public relations continued to soar in the township, we were not doing as well in the business front. We were struggling to make sales as initially envisaged. We worked very hard to push the 60 bottles that we had in stock. Even though we were able to save on accommodation, the sharing arrangement in Kabokweni worked out to less than R100 per head monthly, we were however, spending heavily on transportation and we were running low on cash. We needed to start generating revenue as soon as possible. Moreover, I was under pressure to register for my courses at UNISA. I had secured admission and finally processed my study permit, but I now had to register for my course. Registration for the following academic year would be closed in a few weeks. I had about two weeks to register. I was desperate and wished that I could find a way to sell 8 bottles within the next two weeks. Our agreed commission was R50 per bottle. We decided to stick to the selling price of R100 per bottle - cost price of a bottle was R50.

We kept working the territory and soon the orders started trickling in. Government departments provided the big break we needed. We continued to knock on doors. Rest assured that the more people we saw, the higher our chances of success was. It was the basic law of averages that we had learnt early in the trade. But the more people we saw, the more we were asked about jewellery. Many of the clients would tell us that they would have loved to order some perfumes, but they had just bought some earrings from another Nigerian and are obliged to pay in two monthly instalments. Perhaps we could check back the third month! We eventually got a name and a number and decided it was time to meet up with this brother of ours, who apparently had beaten us to this territory.

We had a permanent spot by Pie City kiosk in the promenade shopping centre where we would gather to have breaks or at the end of the day's work. One of the sales guys, Manelisi, was our good friend. He had tried convincing me to eat one of the pies, but I did not like it. I had issues with the taste of most of the beef. I always ordered drinks and would rather look forward to eating at home. As I made my way to the Pie City kiosk during one of my usual breaks, I noticed that Manelisi was also on break and was seated on one of the benches outside. I noticed that he was busy writing, so I sat beside him and asked what he was doing. He mentioned he was preparing a job application. He asked if I wanted to help him review the application. I had not written any applications in about a year or more but was happy to help with the review.

He was responding to a job advert at a government department for the position of an account officer. I was a little surprised. I did not realize that he had a bachelor's degree and in accounting for that matter. I asked him when he finished university and how long he had been working at Pie City. He had graduated over two years ago and struggled to find a job. He was the only one out of a family of eight kids raised by a single parent, their mum. He had to find a way to support the family and some of his nephews and nieces. I did not think it was difficult for a black South African graduate to get a skilled job. My perception all along was that unemployment only existed in the unskilled job category and that for locals, once you have a degree, you were sought after by all employers looking to fulfil their BEE requirements. I thought only foreigners with qualifications struggled. This was new information for me.

Manelisi and I grew even closer from then onwards. He also came to know that I was also well educated and tried to encourage me to apply for graduate positions as well. I told him I did not have a work permit and besides, I did not think I had much chance of getting a formal employment. I could count how many foreigners were employed in the formal sector. Most were actually doctors who were hugely needed in some of the rural medical facilities. I helped him review many other applications and he eventually found an article position at a branch of the National Auditors Office in Nelspruit.

We met Charles at the promenade. We were hoping to gain more insight into his jewellery business. We were already struggling with the perfumes. We still had over half of our stock unsold after four months in Nelspruit. In fact, Ola had started making regular trips back to Pretoria to service some of his loyal customers who kept calling for orders. I regretted giving up my Tshepo orders as well. I gave in to the temptation and called Tshepo to check on him. Unfortunately, he had been transferred out of the Pretoria office and was now in Durban. It would be a logistical challenge to try to send him stock from Nelspruit. I updated him on my study plans and he wished me well and asked that I stayed in touch. I reached out to other clients and started to use Ola as my delivery liaison as he made his regular trips to Pretoria. All the while, we prayed that Mark and the office would not find out.

It appeared Charles also felt the same way. His business was starting to get a big knock from our activities in the small city. Some of his clients had been hearing about our perfumes and pestered him for some perfumes from his brothers. He struggled to expand his client base as many were already on our books and had very little flexibility in their budgets to accommodate both products. We agreed to work together. We would buy the gold-plated jewellery (earrings, necklaces, and bracelets) that were either imported from Nigeria or directly from France from him at wholesale, and we would sell him the perfumes at wholesale as well. Both parties agreed to stick to the fixed retail price. It was a true Nigerian partnership that worked very well until we left Nelspruit. Having an added product to our line proved very efficient.

We started to increase our revenue and client base at the same time. The jewellery business as we later came to realize, was growing exponentially across the country. At the onset, I could not understand why majority of our clients, black South Africans, could not just go to the mainstream jewellery stores that were widespread in all the retail outlets across the country. I initially thought the ladies loved to support their African brothers, except, that theory was false because the brothers also bought thicker necklaces and bracelets. I later found out that a major factor in the support was a result of the credit record pandemic. Apparently, a significant number of South Africans, disproportionately black South Africans, had adverse credit records and most had been blacklisted and were unable to access credit any longer. What we did invariably, was provide an alternative source of credit for this growing population. We were part

Unjani Mfwethu?

of the solution. We contributed immensely to the advent of the 'bling culture' in Mzansi as it was.

I eventually managed to register for my modules at UNISA. Manelisi was kind enough to give me a loan for two weeks so that I could meet the deadline for the academic year. The University program is structured on a modular basis. The minimum registration amount for my two modules was about R800. All in all, I would have to cover 12 modules to qualify for the postgraduate degree. I was now fully back on course with a renewed sense of purpose. I had been struggling with that feeling of losing one's way and wondering if my education was going to be worth it after all. Starting the new degree, provided me with a great new confidence that flowed into my day job of selling perfumes.

As we continued to work the territory, we got a referral to another city close to Nelspruit. One of Dominique's clients who lived in Barberton, but worked in Nelspruit, had suggested that we try pitching at Barberton as well. She said there were a few businesses and government departments that we may find interesting. Since we had nothing to lose, we decided to give it a shot. Barberton is an old prison town outside of Nelspruit. The bus ride was another hour from Nelspruit and had one of the most thrilling roads and mountains that I have ever seen. It was also the first city where the black township was within a walking distance. I particularly liked the city for its surreal characteristics and traditional homes.

The opportunities were a lot less, as we expected. We had the feeling we had exhausted the city by our second visit. We had secured about four orders already. On the second day and perhaps our last scheduled selling day before returning for deliveries, we walked with two ladies to their offices. It was situated in an old building in the heart of the city. They had seen us pitching to some other ladies in a nearby bakery shop and had asked that we accompany them to their office so they could also have a look.

As we settled into their office, an adjoining door opened, and we could see into a much bigger hall that looked very much like a Home Affairs office. We asked the ladies about it and they confirmed it was Home Affairs. We suddenly became jittery. We always made sure to avoid such establishments given that we did not have any work permits at the time. It was however, too late to make a run for it as the ladies had already helped themselves to the testers. As we continued to steal glances at each other, a man in uniform approached the adjoining door from the inner office and walked towards the ladies. We all waited for the inevitable. The ladies spoke in Ndebele and asked if he did not want to buy for them. He

Unjani Mfwethu?

laughed and stopped to look. "Sanibonani", he said to us - sensing we were foreigners from the manner of our response, he asked how we were. We greeted him in return, and he asked that we come over to his counter once we were done with the ladies, he would like to have a look as well.

For reasons that I still cannot explain, we proceeded to meet with the immigration officer at his counter. He beckoned to us as we approached the quiet hall. He asked if the ladies picked any perfumes, we told him they did not. He smiled and asked if we have any for men. Ola carefully took him through our list of male perfumes, while he sniffed on each tester. Eventually he settled for two bottles of Zeus, Hugo Boss, for delivery and payment on the 21st. We thought among ourselves that he could be trusted. He had appeared very nice and smiling all the time. It is true that selling takes you everywhere, even into the lion's den!

We were back in Barberton on the 21st again. We waited a while for Bongani, the Immigration officer. His colleagues told us that he was in a meeting with the supervisor and asked that we wait. He came out of the meeting after about 30 minutes after waiting and asked that we give him few minutes to attend to some matter. A while later when he arrived, he asked us where we were from. We told him we were Nigerians. Bongani then asked if we did this full time or were we doing other things. Even though it was sounding interrogative, we did not have the feeling he was interrogating us, so we obliged. I told him I was also studying part time and so was Dominique. He asked if we had a work permit... Silence followed. He told us we should apply for one, that he would help us process it. We looked at one another, not able to utter any word. He asked if we were selling for a company and suggested that we get a letter of employment from the company. He got up, picked up his bottles and handed over the cash. He asked us to wait a minute while he went back to his office and returned with three sets of application forms and list of documents. He told us to return the completed forms and documents as soon as possible and with that, we departed. We were too excited to continue any business for the rest of the day. We made our way to the bus station and headed straight back to Kabokweni.

The biggest challenge this time was getting the required employment letter for the work permit application. We were not sure if Chris and Peter would be willing to provide us with such a letter given that we were not employees of the company in the strictest sense. It did not take much persuasion on our part, they agreed to provide the letter but insisted that we restructure the relationship in a way that still reflected some commission-based employment relationship with the company. We submitted the letter with the rest of the documents within two weeks. And true to his word, we received an SMS just three weeks later notifying us that our work permits were now approved. The new permit was a dual permit for work and study. Bongani insisted that we apply for our Permanent Residence immediately. Not that we needed any persuasion, however, we were in shock. How did we move from fearing trading without a permit to the prospect of obtaining a PR? Barberton was a true miracle!

By mid-2003 and during our monthly update with Chris and Peter, they suggested that we look into adding the Eastern Cape to our territories, particularly Port Elizabeth. This resonated well with Dominique. He told us that he knew a Nigerian woman from Pretoria who had a salon in Port Elizabeth. He was willing to give it a try. I still thought I could get more out of Nelspruit in the meantime. By this time, Ola had been leaving for Pretoria more frequently as business was starting to dry up in Mpumalanga. We had also heard the sad news of Mark's suicide. We were all heartbroken. He had been a good boss regardless of how things eventually turned out between us. We prayed that he found eternal peace.

Towards the end of 2003, I found myself somewhat displaced. Larry had left his teaching job in Kabokweni and returned to

Johannesburg where he once again tried to migrate to the UK. He ended up in Asia, I think. Ola was now fully back in Pretoria and Dominque was settling in PE. We had split up the stock by now and each had bilateral access to Chris and Peter. We were technically running individual businesses. I was now without a permanent base. I continued to shuttle between Pretoria, Johannesburg, and Nelspruit. When in Pretoria, I stayed with Ola and two other friends. In Johannesburg, I would spend some time with friends. I continued shuttling for few weeks. I knew I would have to join Dominique in Port Elizabeth but first, I had to check on my PR application in Barberton before travelling to PE. I was now a constant traveller on SA roads.

Ola and I arrived at the Barberton's Home Affairs Office at noon, sometime in late October 2003. To our disappointment, we were told that Bongani was no longer with the department. We were quite surprised given that we had spoken with him just few weeks ago to follow up on our application. We tried his cell number, but it was switched off. We wanted to track our applications, so we asked at the counter for some assistance. The lady directed us to the office of the office supervisor, a Mrs Henriques. She was very warm to us and said Bongani told her about our files. She confirmed that he had left the department and said something about wanting to go back home to family business. Mrs Henriques gave us her direct number to check back in three weeks. She confirmed that our applications were awaiting final approvals. It still felt very unreal. We are on the precipice of getting our permanent residence! What a divine favour that was!

We left the supervisors office and tracked down our old friends in the adjoining room. They knew about Bongani's resignation and advised that we could go to his house in the location. They told us we could not miss it, it was a gigantic white bungalow, we would see it as we approach the township. When we got to the house, there was no one in the building. Being two foreign males, we did not think that it was wise to keep hanging around the township looking suspicious. We left Barberton that afternoon with the hope of catching an evening taxi back to Pretoria.

Ola and I joined Dominique in Port Elizabeth (PE) just before the end of December 2003. PE was a total contrast to Nelspruit. A little rustier compared to Nelspruit but, a much bigger economy. The informal sector was ten times larger than that of Nelspruit, which provided us with a bigger potential for both perfume and jewellery business but bigger competition as well. There was also a bigger migrant population and, in our case, a sizeable Nigerian population.

Dominique had already re-established his relationship with the Nigerian salon owner, Aunty Bola, and by extension, with all her girls – the hairdressers. As much as we really enjoyed the township life back in Nelspruit, it felt good to be back in the city and to be close to the beach. PE offered a different kind of experience.

It did not take long for us to develop a strong client base in PE. Chris and Peter continued to offer great support. They now offered some credit advance on stock purchase as we began to increase our orders. The perfume business grew strongly among the coloured and white population. There were a good number of small businesses in the city which we explored. I had also secured some repeat orders at the UNISA regional office in PE, where I had become a familiar face during registrations and exams inquiries. The jewellery business was also doing very well. We now had multiple suppliers - Aunty Bola and wholesalers travelling in from West Africa and residing in a hotel in Pretoria. These wholesalers would also advance credit to a few select loyal retailers. I started to purchase directly from Nigeria through the post, albeit in smaller volumes, but this direct purchase provided the most margins for me.

The greatest development in PE was, however, the benefit of developing strong relationships with agents and friends who just wanted to assist. I had Hazel at Pick n Pay in Walmer who became a very important agent for my jewellery business - selling over a hundred pieces over the course of two years. There was my very good friend, Mel at the Bay Municipality, who for no payment whatsoever, helped to sell a significant number of jewelleries to her friends and colleagues. Janet, at Fruit and Veg in Newton Park, managed both the perfume and jewellery business at all Fruit and Veg stores in PE, as well as her networks in Motherwell township. Dolly at Ster-Kinekor, Malaika my friend from Kimberley, who taught me valuable lessons in kindness and humanity, and who would help me sell to his fellow students at NMU. Also, my dear landlady at House Electron in North End, who helped to sell at her office. My neighbours, three sisters from Mthatha, who also pushed my products within their networks and at the furniture store where one of them worked.

There were also my Nigerian sisters, hairdressers at Aunty Bola's salon, who also supported in various ways despite their enduring challenges with securing permits. I learnt even more than ever, the importance of relationships in PE. My success depended so much on those various networks, and I never took them for granted. Indeed, I started to imagine a better life in PE and managed to register for and complete a lot more modules at UNISA. Perhaps if I could finish the degree, I might just be able to find a formal job, I thought to myself.

When we arrived in PE, there was already a growing anti-foreigner sentiment and particularly against Nigerians - across the country. These sentiments would reflect in every aspect of our lives. Selling became a little more problematic and I was grateful for the use of intermediaries. One of Mel's colleagues, who bought a pair of earrings and refused to pay, even threatened to call the police on me assuming as usual, that I was in the country illegally. She would stop her car each time she drove past me and would tease me about the earrings. I did not have much time for 'little people'. I was never one to feel cheated in life. I always believed that every experience makes one better.

I remembered a more painful experience at the Western Union Office in Newton Park. I had asked a friend, a Xhosa lady, to assist me in sending some money home through Western Union. All the money transfer agencies by then had restricted non-South Africans or permanent residents with a SA ID from sending money abroad. As soon as we got to the Western Union office, my friend made the necessary enquiries. The attendant, also a Xhosa lady, started to talk to her in isiXhosa. I could tell from the tone of the conversation that things were not going smoothly. Eventually, my friend

Unjani Mfwethu?

turned to me and told me that she will not be able to assist any longer. Apparently, the Western Union officials had frightened her, asking her if she was aware of the risks, she was taking by helping me send money abroad. She had insinuated that the money could have been proceeds of a crime and she could become a complicit in a crime. I was very disappointed, but I understood why my friend could be easily concerned. Carrying the Nigerian Badge of Honour comes with a lot of 'benefits'. It also did not help that there was increasing media attention on Nigerians and drugs at the time. I knew one or two who were involved in certain illicit activities. A neighbour was one of them. I had experienced multiple raids in our block of flats. My landlord and owner of the block and many other flats in PE would always tell me that he hoped I was not going to give him problems like my other countrymen.

Perry was one of the Nigerians who had fled from Durban because of the increasing heat on Nigerians. He was new in the country and wanted desperately to avoid getting involved in any dodgy business. I met him at a KFC joint in North End as I was placing an order. He recognized my accent and immediately greeted me in Nigerian Pidgin English. I was pleasantly surprised to see a fellow Nigerian working in an establishment of such. We became friends and would meet up every now and then to chat. I learnt that his girlfriend, who was also the manager at the restaurant, had gotten him the job. I thought maybe she could help me too. Perry was already becoming restless, he wanted more. He argued that working as an attendant in KFC was not going to make him wealthy. It was not going to buy him the chieftaincy title back in his home village. I could see he was starting to want a different life and could not be bothered about the prospect of rising through the ranks of some fast-food franchise. Sadly, he eventually crossed over to a less desirable business.

We stayed in contact despite his new line of trade. He harassed me about joining his business or at least investing in it to which I would constantly decline and respond that we the 'Yorubas' (people from South west Nigeria) do not engage in such. Perry debunked popular bias that only the 'Igbos' (people from South East Nigeria) were involved in certain crimes at least in South Africa. The bias differs depending on which country and what the makeup of Nigerians in those countries are. He told me categorically, that some of my brothers, fellow Yorubas, professionals and all, were very well involved in his business, and if I did not believe him, he would gladly show me some proof. I was not interested. He argued that all nationalities and people - South Africans, Tanzanians, Ghanaians, Mozambicans, and all Africans for that matter as well as Europeans, Asians, Arabians, and Americans have criminal elements among them and not one nationality can claim monopoly of any crime. I just shrugged, different strokes for different folks. Indeed, many other nationalities are involved in crime in one way or another. Some just seem to be able to stay on under the radar better than others.

Sometimes, Perry would call me at odd hours of the night and on the rare occasions when I picked up, he would joke that I was busy sleeping in South Africa while my people were on the street hustling. He would joke that he would report me to my father. I always responded that unlike him, I was not on a night shift. We would both laugh it off. I remember walking home on an occasion when I saw his car approaching. I was glad to see him, hoping I would get a lift. But as I flagged him down, he looked out and shouted that he was unable to stop as he was being chased by the police. I did not need any more explanation. I immediately jumped to the other side of the road and continued my journey home without drama. That was his preferred life. He eventually relocated to Canada where he promised to return to the straight and narrow way.

Shortly after I arrived in PE, Dominique returned to Pretoria. Ola joined him shortly after. I guess the allure of a bigger city was too much to ignore. Ola and Dominique's cases were different. They had been in Pretoria longer than I and had an entrenched affiliation to the city. I decided to stay back in PE and used the opportunity of being isolated to develop myself further. The isolation afforded me the opportunity of introspection which often required to advance to the next level.

One early morning in June 2004 as I made my way to Hazel in Walmer Park, I suddenly heard a beep on my phone. It was an SMS from the Home Affairs department notifying me that my PR application had been approved. I could not believe my eyes! I had chased Mrs Henriques incessantly with calls and SMSs since the last time in Barberton, asking for any updates. She would always give the same message - awaiting approval. I was beginning to have doubts but kept praying. I immediately called Ola to ask if he got a similar SMS. He did, and so did Dominique. This was a game changer! We immediately made plans to go to Barberton for our permits. I would have to travel up to Pretoria first to meet up with the boys and then onwards to Nelspruit. I called Mrs Henriques to share the good news. She confirmed the approval and asked when we would be coming over.

I wished that I could reach Bongani to share the news and thank him deeply. It is still a mystery that he disappeared

Unjani Mfwethu?

into oblivion shortly after assisting us. Many had written about their personal encounters with angels. This was our encounter in the middle of nowhere. Bongani was our angel, and he was real. We touched him and interacted with him. We even visited his home. We knew his friends. We can all be angels if we choose to be.

CHAPTER 4
The Break of Dawn

Now armed with a permanent residence permit, I decided to go on holiday to visit family and friends back home. It was now almost two years since I left Nigeria. Even though I did not have much money, I had inculcated the habit of 'lay-buys'. It is an old practice, before the credit system took over the world, where one puts down a deposit and then makes regular payments to a merchant to pick up the agreed goods or service at the end of the final payment. I had used the system to acquire several gift items to take with me on my trip back home, and more importantly, for my travel ticket. I was introduced to a travel agent in Pretoria who offered such services to travellers. I was too engrossed with the excitement of going back home and seeing my family to be worried about how little I have saved. I returned to South Africa highly rejuvenated and motivated for the next phase. I was now even more convinced that I had made the right decision leaving in the first place. Things had gotten even more difficult back home for the majority of the people. I did not hide the challenges of leaving one's country to anyone who asked. I wore the hustle proudly on my sleeves and would tell of the opportunities that I envision – even as I continue to find a breakthrough in the new land. My early optimism had not waned a bit. I told myself that I would soon have my degree and hopefully things would start to get a lot better.

My landlord, Des, was not that patient. When I was on holiday, I had arrangements with my agents to intensify their collection efforts from all our clients. I reasoned that even if they only managed to collect 60% of the outstanding money, that would be enough to pay all my outstanding bills by the time I arrived back in South Africa. That was not the case, Hazel complained about delinquent payers and several earrings had been returned due to defects. The most devastating news and setback was the loss of her cousin, who held over R3000 worth of my stock in her possession at the time of her death. I am sure I would not have qualified for any compensation from her life insurance pay-out if there was any at all. I was in a financial hole. I still had to pay the previous month's rent and no prospect of paying the new month's rent either. I also had to pay a few of my suppliers for some of the goods – I knew that I could return the ones with defects but would still be left with a significant debt.

My agents were struggling on all fronts. It was getting increasingly difficult to sell and recover monies from the clients. Competition was now at its highest and forcing prices down tremendously. I was struggling to keep up with monthly bills and could not afford to register for the remaining four modules at UNISA to get my degree. I just needed to make some money for groceries at least. I remember walking to a Fruit and Veg store one morning to try my luck - if Rose would have any money for me. She had been sick for a while and only just returned to work. I knew there were still some monies outstanding from her clients but given that it was her first day back at work, and it was not pay day yet, I did not have many expectations. To my pleasant surprise, she managed to get about R100 from a client who had bought a pair of earrings a month ago. It felt like I had just won the lotto at that moment! I could shop for some groceries and even get some juice. I was glad I listened to my instinct.

I continued to scrap together a few Rands here and there from agents and clients as days went by. I did not have any new stock to distribute, which meant even more trouble as I was only living on past sales without any new sales. I knew I was in deep trouble when I got home one afternoon to a letter from Des. It was an eviction notice - if I did not pay the outstanding rent – a total of R2400. I made about R2000 on a very good month. I was quite desperate and needed divine intervention.

Unjani Mfwethu?

On summer afternoon in February 2005, with the heavy burden of an eviction on my mind, I made my way to UNISA campus in Newton Park using the back road from my flat in North End. I had two bottles of perfumes that Ola had just mailed to me from Pretoria, to deliver to my client. I had agreed with Ola to send me the bottles, since he had on stock, and I would pay him the agreed cost price as soon as I delivered to my client. Sharon was a supervisor at the UNISA regional office in PE. She was one of our loyal clients. I had continued nurturing the relationship after Dominque left, and it helped that I was a student of UNISA.

When I arrived at the UNISA office that afternoon, there was an unusually long queue of students waiting to be assisted. I had to stand aside for few minutes while Sharon and her colleagues attended to the students. I looked at the notice board and saw an advertisement for a position of a Student Liaison Officer. My mind lighted up, and I instantly signalled to Mamake, the elderly office assistant. I asked her about the advertisement and asked if I could apply. She was a little surprised but quickly asked if I met the requirements, which was a mere Matric Certificate. I smiled and said, "Yes, of course". She said, "Oh. In that case, you better apply now as it is the closing day for application". Talk about coincidences! I asked her for a pen and a piece of paper, and immediately handed in my application for the position. I also dropped the two bottles with her to hand over to Sharon. She took my application to Sharon immediately, who gave me a thumbs up and gave Mamake R200 for the perfumes. I left the office happy that I made the sale. I now have an extra R80 in commission for groceries for the week and prayed that I get considered for the position I had just applied for.

Yety had just the other day encouraged me to start applying for more formal jobs, given that the business was no longer promising, and things were starting to get tough. She did not have the negativities I had ingested, listening to the people across the country. I had heard too many negative stories - of even locals unable to secure jobs – that in my innermost; I did not know what to hope for anymore. I just wanted to keep surviving and had even started entertaining the idea of moving on to another country, to Europe or the States. It should be easier now that I had a PR permit.

I was on the road a few weeks after I had submitted my application at UNISA when I got a call from Sharon. It was not the first time that she had called me, so I was not particularly surprised. However, the moment she mentioned my job application, I became very anxious. She told me they had all been surprised at my application, and even more so at my accompanying CV. I had emailed my CV later the same day I submitted my application. They would like to schedule an interview with me as soon as possible. I was even more anxious at the thought of an interview. It would be my first formal interview in South Africa. I did not know what to expect. Yety kept reminding me that these were people that already knew me to a large extent, and I did not have to be anxious. I should just present the best of me. I did not have a tie, so I just wore a formal shirt and pants and made my way to the interview. I kept telling God that His will be done once again.

Des read my employment letter and immediately lighted up. I could tell he was relieved. I am sure he had been worried about the eviction and the odds that I might refuse to go - leading to a costly legal exercise that he was not willing to engage in. He was again reassured that I could now meet my rental liabilities. I told him that I would clear all my existing debts and promised to pay timeously if he would draw up a payment plan. The second call from Sharon few days after my interview, remains one of the best moments of my life. I remember telling Yety when she asked how much I thought UNISA would pay. I had responded that perhaps between R2000 and R3000. My employment letter stated that I was employed on a one-year contract for a monthly salary of R4000. We were ecstatic! It was more than what I had envisaged. I knew this was God intervening again just in time! I was already on a downward spiral and needed a saving grace. It was God telling me in no mistaken manner, that He would always be there. I vowed to make the most of the opportunity.

Working at UNISA provided a glimpse into a life in South Africa's formal sector. It opened a different door for me. It provided a platform from which I could reach for even greater things. The UNISA regional office in PE was a small office. There were about eight staff members. Three of us were contract staff while the remaining five, were permanent staff. I was one of three student liaison officers. We were responsible for all student matters - from admissions to registration, examinations, fees, and graduation. I reported to Sharon who in turn, reported to the regional head. I was glad that I had done a one-year computer science certificate course in Nigeria before travelling. The program included courses on computer software usage and computer networking. This skill would come handy during my time at UNISA. Given the size of the office, we had to be hands-on and improvised on most things - from routine IT issues to courier and document management.

I was always the first to arrive at work in the morning. I would leave home early enough for my thirty minutes' walk to the office every day, and soon assumed the responsibility of keeping the office keys, so I could let myself in every morning. I was passionate about my work and made sure I understood both the letters and spirit of the student guidelines. I developed good relationships with colleagues at the head office in Pretoria, as well as with my students - many of whom today are still friends. I was shocked to see one of them at my church a while back, when I had moved back to Pretoria. It did not take long to become a great resource to my colleagues and supervisors.

There were always long queues of students, young and mature, waiting in line to see me. Many would insist that they only wanted me to attend to them, sometimes to the annoyance of my colleagues. Often during these instances, Sharon would step in to move the lines and assure the students that they would get same level of service. The phones were no different. I received calls after calls, especially during registration periods, asking to speak to the Nigerian guy.

I helped many who otherwise, would have been told that they do not qualify, to take some courses or to even register. Foreigners alike wanted only to consult with me. They knew I would not just turn them away but would seek for solutions. I would use my contacts at the head office to get guidance on many issues that even my supervisors could not assist on. Sharon would refer many cases to me for assistance. She was one of a kind, never too proud to ask for my guidance whenever she found herself stuck on some guidelines. I guess I benefited immensely from my ability to process large information quickly and build relationships with stakeholders. She was also conscious of the fact that I was studying for a postgraduate degree and thought that must have been the reason for my 'intelligence'. She only had a diploma at the time and would tell anyone who cared to listen, that I was an extremely smart person. I did not think so, given my struggles. I thought she was just being very kind. I was just glad to have been given the opportunity to work. The least I could do, was do it to the best of my ability and with all honesty. And if by so doing, I managed to dispel some of the stereotypes against foreigners, even better.

I made many friends in my position at the office. I was perhaps one of the most popular UNISA staff at many of PE's corporate offices and government departments. I also became popular even among fellow foreigners. My colleagues would always refer all foreigners to me. I took care of them all. I even got an offer from one of my 'brothers' who had made an inquiry about admission. He had observed that I was also in charge of student payments. I took details of copies of student credit cards for payments. This to my brother represented a 'quick rich' opportunity. He tried to lure me into providing him copies of these documents for a handsome reward. I told him with a straight face never to ask me such a thing again.

There were many other foreigners who inspired me. I met many who were professionals and furthering their studies. Some were bankers, doctors, and lawyers who either wanted to do their MBA or studying for a second degree. I enjoyed chatting with them to learn about their experiences - how they got their jobs, and all their stories gave me hope. Many of my South African clients also started developing more interest in my personal story. Some even offered to assist with jobs at their companies.

One of my students, a Ugandan, was working with Standard Bank at the time. I always liked his disposition. He appeared very comfortable and his employers paid in full for his MBA. I asked him about his job and how he got to join the bank. He told me that he applied for the graduate program immediately after finishing at Wits University. He encouraged me to apply for the program as well and gave me the link. It was a very long online application form. I had to complete lengthy psychometric tests and fill out my CV online. I stayed back every day at work for three days to complete it. It felt good to envision working at a bank in South Africa.

The rainy seasons were particularly hard. I stuck to walking to and from work every day so I could save on transportation cost. I also packed my lunch to work daily. Some of my colleagues would tease me as they placed orders for some of the popular fast foods. I just ignored the jokes most of the time. Majority of my colleagues then, were still living at home with their parents. One of my student clients became a very good friend. She worked at the state broadcasting network and later, joined a car manufacturing company. She would always give me a lift home anytime she drove past me. She was very ambitious and was keen to obtain more degrees.

As our contracts came close to an end by late 2006, Sharon called a meeting and informed us of a major change in UNISA's regional office structures. Some offices were going to be shut down, while some would be reduced to satellite offices with lean staff. Affected permanent staff across the country, would either be integrated into the head office structures or given severance packages. She said it was a moment of great uncertainty among all staff. Even she was not sure what would happen to her. She did not think that our contracts would be renewed.

I did not have much time to wallow in self-pity. I knew I had to intensify my search for a new job. I also only had two more

Unjani Mfwethu?

modules to complete in just three months before obtaining my postgraduate degree, which would hopefully enhance my employability. I was also motivated by the Standard Bank application. Even though I had not been selected for the next round, the process had ignited in me a stronger desire to get into corporate SA. I went on a frenzy of job applications. I must have applied to no less than 30 companies, when I eventually got an interview with Cell C in Cape Town through the agency that advertised the job. My colleagues and Sharon were very excited, and all felt confident that I would get the job. Sharon stood ready to provide a good reference for me whenever required. She had lived in Cape Town and told me how beautiful it was.

I was to bear the entire cost of the interview, but I did not mind. The prospect of working with a telecoms company in Cape Town was exhilarating. There was only one person that I knew in Cape Town. She used to live in PE and worked at Ster-Kinekor. I called her and told her about my job interview in Cape Town. I was going to travel by bus overnight and wanted her assistance in navigating my way from the bus station to the interview venue.

I arrived in Cape Town at dawn, met up with Dolly, who took me to the train station in the CBD where I quickly freshened up at the gents and changed into proper clothes for the interview. We had a quick breakfast at the station and then made our way to the Cell C office for my 09:00 interview. I met the job agent at the interview site and she quickly brought me up to speed on what to expect. There were eight applicants for the position of Customer Support Officer. The company had decided to complete the interview that same day to accommodate those of us who had travelled from other regions. They planned to have three stages of the interview. A written test and two oral interviews - one was a role play. I thought to myself that this was going to be intense. The salary expectation was between R8000 and R10 000. The thought of what I could do with that much money was in itself, motivating.

At the end of the interview, I felt very confident that I had done quite well, especially given that only three of us had made it to the final round. It was exhausting, but I thought I had a compelling story to tell in sales and customer service. Above all, I trusted in God. After saying goodbye to Dolly and thanking her for her hospitality, I got into the bus to PE, ready for another all-night journey back home. I knew everyone would be waiting to hear the outcome. The agent had promised to let me know as soon as she got feedback.

Unjani Mfwethu?

The feedback came sooner than I imagined, barely 10 minutes into the journey. We had just approached Century City when my phone rang, it was my agent. She told me that she had both good and bad news and wanted to know which I would prefer to hear first. I chose to hear the bad news first. She told me that I did not get the job, but that the good news was that all the interviewers thought I was by far the best candidate they had seen in a long time. They felt that I was overqualified for the role and I would not stay long in the role or in the company before I am head hunted. They said they would employ me for a senior role if there was an opening and that they would like to keep my details on file for future openings. I was deflated! I did not understand how any of the news was good. I begged my agent to go back to the client and tell them that I would not leave the company if given a chance. I asked her to let them know that I love the role and was passionate about customer service. I was even ready to sign an undertaking to that effect. I was desperate for the job. How could I be overqualified? I had paid my way to the interview, travelled overnight for the role. I really needed the job. My UNISA contract was ending in few weeks.

I looked out of the bus window as we drove further north of the city. I could see the mountains behind us and the beautiful lights adorning the highway and buildings. I longed to be in Cape Town. I said to myself quietly that I would be back. I took out my phone and made two phone calls, one to Dolly and another to Yety. I stretched out my legs on the City-to-City bus and slept the entire night.

The PE UNISA office became a satellite office with only three staff members. Sharon, Mamake and the regional head were the only three retained. The rest of us were let go. I managed to get an extra month with UNISA's research council, to help with a survey program. I was very grateful for the extra one-month income while I continued to look for a job. I dreaded going back to the days of hawking and instability of income. Des had been very nice to me since I got the UNISA job. I did not want to upset the relationship.

Sometime late 2006, about a month after I finished the one-month contract with UNISA and deciding not to go back to my old business, I got a call for an interview with an international advertising company based in Johannesburg. I remember reading the job advertisement online and getting excited about the job. I applied for a Marketing Officer post. The role would include lots of travelling, both domestic and international. One of their new markets was Nigeria. I imagined myself representing them in Nigeria and tailored my application specifically in that line, making sure to highlight my Nigerian roots and connections.

I was quite pleased when I received the call for an interview in Johannesburg – and again, at my own cost. I did not mind at all. It would also be an opportunity to meet up with my friends. It had been over a year since we saw one another. I was very excited about the journey. I got a My City-to-City bus ticket and got ready for the journey. The day I left; I received another email from an asset management company in Cape Town, Allan Gray. They had received my application for the graduate program and wanted to schedule an interview with me. They wanted to know where would be best to conduct the interview. They had centres in East London and Graham's town in the Eastern Cape, and since I was going to be passing through Graham's town on my way from Johannesburg, I thought it best to opt for Graham's town. I was not very keen on the company even though it was Cape Town. The city I had fallen in love with and had vowed to return to, did not seem too enticing because I was too fixated on the advertising company and prospects of Nigeria travels. I had very little time to consider another company. But yes. I committed to the interview.

For some odd reason, the interview with the Ad agency did

not seem to go the way I hoped it would. There were too many technical questions about advertising and marketing that I could not answer properly. It became apparent during the interview, that I may not be qualified for the job even though I had the advantage of being Nigerian. They confirmed that it was a market they were looking to enter and being a Nigerian, was definitely an advantage. They promised to get back to me.

The remainder of my time in Joburg went very well. I had great fun visiting friends and spent a night in Pretoria before making my way back again to the Eastern Cape. I confirmed from the City-to-City bus company if I could break my journey in Graham's town on the same ticket. That was great news to me. I did not have to buy a new ticket from Graham's town to PE. Given the way that the interview with the Ad Agency had gone, I started to give more thoughts about the next interview. Yety had googled the company and seemed to like it. I also did some research and read up on asset management and basics of investing on the bus - even though I had no background in finance.

Notably, Allan Gray was kind enough to arrange a hotel for me so I could properly freshen up, have a decent breakfast, and maybe, even a short nap before my interview later in that

Unjani Mfwethu?

morning. It was my first time at Rhodes University. I had seen pictures and watched videos of the Oxford University in England, and Rhodes appeared to be very similar to what I had seen of Oxford University. The ancient but solid buildings looked stunning even amid the obvious poverty of its surrounds. My hotel had similar allure. It was a converted prison. My windows still had the prison bars, and the doors were made of steel with the iron bars still intact. Even the single bed and bath, even though very modern, were inspired by a prison style. I was very impressed. It would be my closest to luxury and pampering since I arrived in the country.

My interview was scheduled for 11:00 am but I was too anxious to sit around in the room. I made my way to the interview venue in one of the university buildings. The lady at the reception hall reminded me that I was an hour early and I told her not to worry about it. I am happy to wait, and so I sat looking at the giant reception hall. After about 20minutes, I saw a middle-aged white lady walk out of one of the rooms and wandering around. I could hear her muttering to the other lady and then pointing at me. The middle-aged lady walked towards me and asked if I was her 11:00 am appointment. I answered, and she said, "Oh well, you might as well come in now. The 10:00 am appointment is late".

It was a long interview, but mostly conversational. Hannah, my interviewer, asked lots of questions and dug deeper into my personal story. She wanted to know more about my selling experience and times where I may have showed leadership and independent thinking. I got a sense she was quite impressed with what I had to say. I remember her partying words to me on the day: "I am glad you were early".

I arrived in PE that evening with Allan Gray's glossy brochure in hand. Yety later told me that the moment she saw the brochure, she wished that I would be employed at the company. The brochure was exceptionally elegant. If it was anything like what the company was like, then she wanted me to be there. I just wanted a job quickly.

I received another call from Allan Gray two weeks later inviting me for a final interview in Cape Town - they paid for my flight as well. Memories of my first trip came flooding back. It was strange that just few months after my last visit, I would be returning to the city for another interview. Dolly could not believe that I was interviewing with Allan Gray. Apparently, she knew more about the company than I did. She said it was one of the most prestigious companies to work for, and that I must have really impressed them.

I did not know what to believe. I was just getting to know the ins and outs of South Africa's corporate world. It was not like I had been thinking of a company to manage my money prior to then. I knew the big four banks and particularly, Standard Bank because it was the first image I had of my corporate dream. Anything beyond that was unknown to me or my world then. I did not know what medical aids were, or insurance companies until UNISA and even then, I did not get any of those benefits. I only knew that my other colleagues who were permanent staff, were on some sort of medical aid and retirement funds. At the time, my world was less complicated. I just needed to pay my rent and buy groceries. I even wished I could be refunded all my UIF contributions which proved too difficult to retrieve during the time I was out of job. It was easier to go back to selling than spending hours going back and forth from the labour office.

I arrived at Cape Town International airport and was transported to Allan Gray's offices at the Victoria and Alfred (V&A) Waterfront by a designated shuttle driver. For some reason, the Cape Town I was visiting now, seemed different from the one I had come to previously admire. It was brighter, more stunning and had a very cosmopolitan vibe to it. When I mentioned this to Dolly, she laughed and ascribed my feeling to the 'change' in my circumstances. She said I was now experiencing Cape Town from the lens of the rich and mighty. I laughed and dismissed her. I admitted quietly to myself that she was right. One cannot totally dismiss the difference of waking up on a bus, to a crowded station. I recognize that this time, I was travelling like an elite.

I was interviewed by a three-person panel, including Hannah who gave me a wide smile as I made my way into the interview room. I repeated some of the stories that I told earlier and was asked a lot more technical questions around client services, finance, investments, and sales. I was a bit more nervous this time around. While the first interview was a lot more relaxed, given then I was not as invested as I was now, the second interview was filled with nerves. I knew what was at stake, and I was in love with Cape Town and had been showed a taste of what working with a good corporate entailed. I wanted it!

After the interview, one of the panellists took me on a tour of the building and then out through a back exit to the most astonishing piece of property called, the V & A Waterfront. It was nothing like anything I had ever seen! It was a mall, dockyard, entertainment centre all rolled into one. She pointed out to the stunning Table Mountain backdrop and asked if all of that was something that I could consider leaving PE for? I was too stunned to say anything. I left for the airport completely hypnotized. I prayed every minute of the way that I get the job. This time carefully omitting the phrase 'God's will be done'. I just assumed it had to be His Will too. The panellists had told me that they would get in touch with me before the end of that week. It would be the longest week of my life.

It really was the longest week. I began to grow anxious as the days went by without any call or email. When Friday arrived, and still no feedback, I prepared myself for the worst and imagined my hopes being dashed once again. Yety remained strong and continued to hold onto her strong belief that the job was mine. I was not so sure, especially when I checked the time again and it was 16:00 on the day. I had practically been watching the hands of the clock move all day long. Earlier in the day, I had asked Yety to go to campus to help check my emails in case they had sent an email, but she found nothing.

At exactly five minutes before five pm on that Friday, I received a call from Angela, the Head of Client Services. I remember lying on the carpet of my living room. She asked if I had been waiting long for the call. It took all my strength to remain calm. She said calmly that they would like to offer me the job, and she waited for a reaction. It was complete silence... I looked at Yety and she knew immediately what the call meant. She asked if I was still on the line and I replied quickly saying yes. I started to thank her and everyone at the company. She described how she and Hannah had fought over me. She had wanted me for her own department, Client Services, but Hannah was so impressed with me that she had insisted that they offer me a much higher role in the new elite team she was running. A team which managed the affairs of the company's ultra-high net worth clients, private clients. She added that there was a catch. I had to achieve distinctions in my remaining two papers, which I was due to write in December that year. I did not know if she was serious or not, but I knew I would not give her or the company any reason to deny me the great opportunity to join the company.

My exams were just three weeks away. I began studying like I had never studied before, even though I had always been very successful in my other papers scoring very good grades. I had resolved since registering at UNISA to approach my studies differently from my first degree back home. I wanted to distinguish myself through education in this new land.

Unjani Mfwethu?

And even as it appeared that I was taking longer than usual to complete my postgraduate due to lack of finances, I persevered.

So yes, I studied extra hard and as God would have it, I achieved the required distinctions in the two papers. One was just by the margins but a distinction, nonetheless. The results would reinforce in me what I had always known to be one of my strengths: to study and pass exams when I choose to. I would always prescribe education and excelling at it, to every migrant that I know. I remember telling my younger brother who moved to the UK for his postgraduate studies, that he should do all that he can to achieve excellence in his studies – not that he needed to do a lot in that regard, he is gifted. Academic excellence is a tried and tested path to quick stability in any new country. I am aware there are many other paths.

When I went to the UNISA office to pick up my official statement of my results as required by Allan Gray, I met Sharon and the Regional Head, Mr Payne. They were very happy to hear the good news. Mr Payne assured me that I would really enjoy working at Allan Gray and that the company has a great reputation. They would take good care of me. That was very good to know. I told myself that if Mr

Payne knew so much about Allan Gray, then it must truly be a good company.

I was very excited and looked forward to this new chapter of my life. God is truly awesome!

CHAPTER 5
Homecoming

Life in Cape Town and at Allan Gray was on a different level. Cape Town is an extraordinarily beautiful city and continues to rank as one of the best cities in the world. The city is completely different from other South African cities, not least because of its very cosmopolitan make-up. It is no wonder that many in South Africa, especially the black community, often joke that one will require a visa to visit Cape Town. It does feel like a totally different country sometimes.

Allan Gray fitted well into the ambience of the city. The company was everything that I had been told it would be. I felt welcomed from my first day. Perhaps due to its relatively small staff strength, everyone felt a sense of belonging. The COO knew almost everyone by name. It was a close-knit family - you appreciate the company even more once you are out of it. It is why, despite its high staff turnover rate, it has the highest record of ex-staff returning to the company, which makes its net-staff turnover almost negligible.

I had many memorable moments in the city, and really

enjoyed my time with Allan Gray. It was blessed with many company-sponsored family getaways at many of Western Cape's finest. I am unable to forget the luxurious dinner organized by the Cape of Good Hope on the renowned Table Mountain and graced by South African celebrities, top of which was Bishop Desmond Tutu. The magic of having five hundred VIP guests along one table at the heart of Table Mountain, was beyond spectacular!

During this time, I learnt the world of finance and investments, and picked up two additional degrees in the process. Living in Cape Town also exposed me, more than in any other South African city, to the contradictions of the South African economy. This is better observed when driving from the Cape Town Airport into town - where the optical transition from the deplorable habitations, along the highway into the first world type structures, leaves every first-time visitor in a state of wonder. Cape Town is also a city with less migrants compared to the other big cities in South Africa. This could be the reason I experienced less incidents of Xenophobia. One is more likely to experience real or perceived racism, as a black person in Cape Town, than Xenophobia I would say. But in general, I found Cape Town a little more accommodating (although my local friends would always disagree with me on this part). However, I must confess that despite my relatively good experience in South Africa, there were moments when I actually second guessed my decision to stay in South Africa given the growing negative sentiments and prejudices.

I made lots of new friends, mostly white and coloured people, in Cape Town, which gave me rare insights into the other 'world'. I remember lengthy and deep conversations around race and culture that I had with friends across the aisle during dinner meetings. I assume many of my hosts found it less delicate to discuss such issues with me - given that I was not a black South African whom they perceived as sometimes too emotional. I, on the other hand, benefitted from the openness of our conversations, using the opportunities to understand a little better, the minds of the 'oppressor' in the case of my white friends. Moreover, in the case of my coloured friends, the minds of the 'oppressed' in both pre and post-Apartheid era.

There is a strong sense of mutual suspicion on all sides based on personal experiences and history, and nowhere is this suspicion greatly elevated, than in the corporate world. The few black migrants who were lucky enough to make it into the corporate world, were usually the neutral ones. They are often faced with the pressure of picking sides. The whites looking to use them to prove their non – racist genes, while the locals, resent the fact that these migrants are just seemingly content to have a job and would do everything to impress their benefactors. The African migrant is merely a pawn. Both the local black South African and white South Africans watch each other like hawks. Theirs is a long unending battle, and the African migrant would be better off with a policy of non-alignment. However, this is easier said than done. A careful look at many official gatherings or so called 'Friday drinks', will reveal the natural separation of the 'colours' of this 'rainbow nation'. The local blacks on one side, whites on another, and the coloureds on another. The African migrants finds themselves hovering all around, struggling to find a permanent ally. I would later observe similar dynamics in the USA – with the African Americans, white Americans, and the African migrants.

Based on my observation, the tensed relationship between the foreigners and the locals, can be traced to the antics used mostly by the white folks in disparaging the local blacks. Very often, local blacks have been compared to the African migrants – who are hardworking, more enterprising, and less angry, neglecting that, migrants all over the world have an extra motivation to take up any kind of jobs and are often more grateful for any handouts or opportunities provided them by the host country or people. They have only learnt to accept their realities as foreigners and put aside any sense of entitlement, be it as it may, at least until such times when they start to feel a bit more settled and integrated. Migrants are therefore, seen as vulnerable groups. For this reason, they have profited tremendously from the help and activities of several NGO's representing the interests of migrant groups.

This unfair comparison, coupled with the migrants desperate attempt to survive, continues to ire the locals who feel undermined in their collective bargaining efforts with their employers. This interplay is not limited to the formal sector, the same dynamic can be observed in the informal sector. Just as I took to the business of selling perfumes when I first arrived in the country, many other migrants, including Asians, were engaged in several other forms of small businesses. A large majority were also employed in the farming, logistics, and mining sectors as cheaper labour.

I received great insights on this issue from my very good friend and a South African, who has demonstrated time and time again, her loyalty and love to me and my family. She shed some light on some of the root causes of the anti-foreigner sentiments among many black South Africans (including the Coloured and Asian communities as well). According to her, the anti-foreigner sentiments can be traced in part to the desperation of foreigners to earn a living at all cost, even if it meant being exploited by the oppressors. When I tried to argue that the African migrant is not the enemy and perhaps it was time for black South Africans to stop with the blame game and hold their destinies in their hand, she admonished me for oversimplifying the black or non-white South African struggle. I was told that I was too naïve, and that if none of my parents have had to clean the floors of the oppressors, wash their clothes, and tend their gardens, then I did not have any right to judge a black South African.

Contrary to what employers may say, migrants are not biologically wired differently to the locals. If one considers for a moment domestic migration, one can see clearly that even locals who have had to move from one province to another, are immediately seen as threats to other locals in the new province. Even though these migrants are nationals of the same country. Xenophobia – a natural consequent of migration – is a universal phenomenon and attributed largely to economic issues. There is something to be said about xenophobia. Xenophobia in simple terms, refers to the act of discriminating against people from other countries or nations. It is a deplorable act, much like racism, that affects everyone involved in many adverse ways. It is rooted in fear and ignorance and seeks to spread division and hatred among people.

It is a very heart-breaking experience being on the receiving end of Xenophobia. Often, the world and national leaders, only notice the occasional outbreaks of Xenophobic attacks, but pays little attention to the more subtle, day to day Xenophobia being experienced by migrants in the country. In South Africa, Xenophobia predates 1994, even though on a relatively smaller scale. There were reported cases of anti-foreigner sentiments pre 1994 in the mining industry, which had a large proportion of migrant workers from neighbouring countries. Xenophobia, however, became more prevalent post 1994 as more African migrants made their way to the 'Free South Africa'. This influx of African migrants into the country, became noticeable as the hopes of freedom began to wane, coming to a head during the global economic meltdown of 2007/2008.

It is hard living in a country where you are constantly interrogated. Every conversation and interaction with the locals can easily turn into an 'interrogation'. Everyone would want to know where you are from, what do you do, when do you plan to return home? On one occasion, I was at a branch office of a bank to replace my damaged ATM card. I observed with familiarity, how the attendant's countenance changed the moment I responded to him in English, and even more so, when he saw the name on my card. I guess he could not help himself, as he immediately became interrogative. He asked if I was Nigerian, where I was before coming to South Africa and how long I have been in the country. It was very appalling, given that he reeked of so many stereotypes. When he found out that I was banker, he then did what many would do, try to be condescending by saying that he could see that I chose the straight and narrow path unlike many of my countrymen.

I remember the story shared by a colleague who was born in South Africa to a South African mother and Zimbabwean Father. She had gone into a retail store in Cape Town, and after presenting her SA ID, the attendant asked how she got her ID and how much she paid for it. It appears every local South African is a trained immigration officer. Even a domestic help that I was going to employ, quickly turned the interview on me as soon as she picked up on my accent over the phone. She wanted to know where I was from. She did not want to work with Nigerians.

Unjani Mfwethu?

Experiences with some law enforcement officers are no different. A friend had escorted a family member to the airport when he was approached by a police officer who demanded to see his ID. When he complied and presented his ID, the police officer grabbed it in annoyance and tore it into two pieces, in the full glare of everyone around. He blurted out without any proof whatsoever, that the ID was forged, and he did not give a damn about it. As to be expected, my friend was enraged and caused a big scene at the airport. The police officer was later remanded. But such is the manner of treatment bestowed upon migrants of African descent. You are first and foremost a fraud before anything else. As a matter of fact, very few really understand the difference between legal and illegal migrants.

The harassments and interrogations get to a point where you can no longer distinguish between genuine interests in your well-being, just mere mischief, or xenophobia. The result is that one develops albeit unconsciously, an innate defensiveness to every question that is deemed private. In any case, xenophobia is not limited to the black South African. Even some white South Africans, would indulge in some xenophobia themselves too. I once received a call from a white South African client, who told me he was curious about my accent, and wanted to know my origin. When I told him I was Nigerian, he sighed, and made a wry joke that I must be the only Nigerian not in jail. The harassments were just too overwhelming, and sometimes when other non-South African whites want to appear sympathetic, they would ask how I was coping with being a Nigerian in South Africa. They thought that it must be hard enough being black. I remember a time when I was on a business trip to a European country, one of my colleagues joked that at least in Europe, I did not have to worry about xenophobia but only racism. In Europe, every black person was African. It did not matter from which part of Africa. But in Africa, you are not black. You are Nigerian, Zimbabwean, Tanzanian, Ghanaian or whatever the case may be.

Again, the more frightening part of xenophobia in South Africa is that it is not restricted to the poor and uneducated only. For some reason, the sentiment seems to have permeated through all ranks of the society. It is of no surprise that even the leadership of the country, often found it difficult to have a unified voice against acts of xenophobia and be quick to condemn the attacks when it happens. There is a differing view on how to treat the issue of migration and how to treat migrants. On many occasions when I would engage with

Unjani Mfwethu?

some of my black South African colleagues at work on issues of xenophobia, I would end up being shocked to hear that their position was no different from the views on the street and in townships. My colleagues contended that why would anyone want to remain in a country that does not want them. They argued that it was best for the foreigners to leave, alas not the European investors, as they refer to the white migrants, but the African migrants.

The only group of people who did not care much about migrants were the coloured population. For some unexplainable reasons, they never felt any animosity towards African migrants or if they did, never really showed it - except for general cases of anti-drug concerns and raids in the Western Cape and Cape Flats. The South African whites, for the most part, are just too elated for the distraction from the regular 'war cries' from the South African blacks. They benefit from the new 'enemy', who besides being a welcomed distraction, is also a cheaper source of labour.

There is an anonymous quote that, when you exist in a space that was not built to accommodate you, being you is the revolution. It is exactly how I perceive my South African journey. Living in South Africa shone a big bright light on the widening level of socio-economic disparity in the world's large issues of race, ethnicity, sexual identity, age, disability, income, and geographic location which have become more pronounced. The numerous stereotypes that we hold of one another as groups or class of people did not do much to ameliorate the disparity. White, black, and brown we all carry some level of bias - a popularly held idea or belief about each other that often gives rise to incidents of racism and xenophobia. Even though this oversimplified image of another in our minds, may enable us to respond rapidly to situations, it makes us ignore the differences between us as individuals. While some are unaware of these innate biases, others actively give life to it, and propagate all manners of stereotypes unapologetically so.

Many stories have been told about racism, and how the white race as a collective, often struggles with this challenge. There are indeed many unrepentant racists around the world and in South Africa. They make no attempt to hide their disgusting behaviour. Many of these racists demand submissiveness from the black person. They are happy when a black person 'remains in his or her lane'. It is totally inconceivable to imagine a non-white person as an equal. These are the slave owners and their descendants. There are those who argue that they are not racists, even if their actions or words constitute racism. They are the ones who quickly tell you how many black friends they have. They minimize the black person's struggle and will often want you to move on quickly and let the past be in the past. They are the ones that make racist jokes but do not expect any backlash because according to them, they are not racists.

I remember just having completed my Certified Financial Planning (CFP) program, and the results had come out during work hours. When I checked my email and found out I had gotten a distinction, I could not contain my excitement. It had been a very tough year of studying. My colleagues were curious and rushed to my computer to see what the news was about, including one of my bosses who happened to be on the floor at the time. When he heard about my result and the grades, which by the way was the best result among all five of us, he cynically asked if the CFP exam I had written was a junior CFP. Such unguided remarks speak to a suppressed or hidden perception about the black person. It appears to be an expectation of underperformance by the black person, so much so, that once a black person exceeds these expectations, they almost qualify to sit at the table with the white folks. It is common to hear remarks such as 'oh, you are so different'. I always found such comments resentful. I would ask, different from what exactly?

We get so wrapped up in all the stereotypes that even when we have good intentions, they are easily misconstrued by the other, and sometimes stereotyping could even lead to unintended consequences in some cases. I recall three separate but related incidents.

The first was at my place of work in Cape Town. My boss called me into the meeting room on one occasion and mentioned that she would like me to go for voice training. My guard was up immediately. I asked if anything was wrong with my voice. In my mind, it sounded like one of those racially motivated suggestions. I became defensive and told her sternly that I was proud of my Nigerian accent and did not see why she would want me to sound like someone else. I guess she must have anticipated my reaction as she was quite calm, even as I went on and on. She reassured me of her good intentions, and that she really was not trying to make me sound 'white' as I thought. She only wanted to provide me with the tools to do my job even more efficiently. She told me that she also did the training some years back and found it extremely useful. The training was designed to help with better enunciation and speech control. That made sense to me. I did not have any reason to think that she was lying about the intentions, even though the African in me still did not like the sound of enunciation and speech control

Unjani Mfwethu?

very much. I felt strongly that the way I spoke, with all its imperfections was after all, my identity. But again, I was not averse to further developments. I enrolled for the training and really loved it. It again proves that when we speak to one another openly and without dismissal, we are able to understand one another and learn from each other.

The second episode was in front of my house. Another classic case of how we get caught up in stereotype that could endanger the lives of others. On this notable day, I was standing outside my property watching as my son rode his bicycle from a distance. A private security operative drove past me. Within twenty seconds of seeing him drive past, I received a call from my private security company. The caller told me that they had just received a call from one of their response team - there was a black man standing in front of my house with the garage door opened. I wished someone had been around to capture my look at that instant on video. I did not know if I should laugh or be upset, but I remember being calm and telling the lady that I was grateful for the call. However, the black man standing in front of the property happens to be the owner of the property, which also happens to be me. I can only imagine her embarrassment at that moment. She went very quiet and quickly apologized for the error. I later called the area manager and invited him over to my property so he could tell his team that yes, there is a black property owner on the street, so that I do not get confused as an intruder. The incident reminded me of a Hollywood movie, of a black man being arrested in his home and charged with breaking and entering.

The third was at the airport. I am usually very defensive when going through immigration at OR Tambo. Some of the immigration officers, mostly blacks, always find pleasure in harassing foreigners, especially those who happen to hold South African Passports. One even insinuated, while struggling to find a free page in my passport, that I was enjoying his country but more so, the women. I usually just ignored such remarks. So, yes, I always put up my non-chatty look when approaching the immigration officers. On this day, the officer held onto my passport a little too long. He looked at me and asked if I spoke any local South African languages, and if I knew what languages were on the South African currency note. I was very confused, not knowing where the conversation was headed, and the purpose of the question. I told him I did not speak any and that I had no idea what other languages were on the note besides English. He would not give up and asked if I had any South African notes on me. By this time, I was getting more curious. I gave him a R20 note and he read out some words in Zulu that are inscribed on the note. He told me as a South African, I needed to know which language was represented on South African money. We both laughed and I promised him that I would make sure to study the notes henceforth. It was the first time that a black South African openly acknowledged me as a South African. I felt bad for having initially put up a wall and not giving him a chance as an individual. Sometimes, our prejudices are born out of lack of knowledge or exposure.

In the early Eighty's in Nigeria, there was a widespread anti-foreigner sentiment particularly towards our West African neighbours, especially Ghanaians. The truth was that majority knew very little about the people across the borders because of very little cross border trades and travels between these countries. This changed drastically in the Ninety's, as Nigerians found themselves travelling more to West African countries for trade and for educational purposes for their children. Ghanaian schools became the preferred option for Nigerian middle class. Even though, xenophobia was not totally eradicated, the increasing trade and travel helped to dispel many of the age long stereotypes among the respective people. Xenophobia has a direct correlation with economic activities. As an economy grows, causing significant decadence in poverty rates and unemployment, anti-foreigner sentiments will also start to wane. The challenge for leaders is to create an economy that accommodates both locals and foreigners - one that maximizes the benefits of immigration.

The deadly 2008 nationwide xenophobic attacks in South Africa broke my spirit. It was extremely scary and depressing to watch images of fellow Africans being chased, attacked, mobbed, some burnt alive, and the harrowing cries of women and children. It was hard to imagine any African that did not feel the pain and fear of the moment. It was this single event that finally hit home for me - it does not matter how long you have been in the country; you are always a foreigner and an unwanted foreigner no matter your status. It was very disheartening. I received incessant calls from family and friends from far and wide. They had all seen the horrific images being broadcast across the globe and wanted to know if we were safe. It was increasingly difficult to ignore the hostility and the imminent danger that hung in the air. My parents wanted us to return home immediately. But I have never been the one to act out of fear. I maintained that I would monitor the situation and act accordingly - reassuring them that we were far away from the whole fiasco, and that it was largely restricted to the townships.

The seeds had been sown. I knew then that I had to start thinking strongly about returning home but would have to plan it properly. It is not easy packing up after nine years in the country. I needed to prepare mentally and financially – part of which meant that I needed to have a plan for a job in Nigeria. I had no strings to pull back home to get me a desired job, I decided to focus on opportunities in South Africa that could provide me with a position in Nigeria or West Africa. I narrowed my plans down to two. They were both very ambitious plans, but this would not be my first time plotting big.

The first plan was to try and persuade my current employer to consider opening a Nigerian office, with the hope that I will be appointed as the Country Manager or any other position in Nigeria. The second plan was to search for other South African businesses or multinationals domiciled in South Africa, which also have a local presence in Nigeria. I would proactively approach these businesses for a job in their Nigerian office. The first plan was more elaborate.

I had to do a lot of background market research showcasing the benefits of an expansion to Nigeria. This was at a time when Nigeria was not yet the flavour of the moment for many South African businesses, so it was really a hard sell, but I did not buckle. I enlisted the support of a trusted colleague and friend, who was very skilled in matters of strategy. We developed quite an impressive idea, which was presented to the top management of the company. The COO, however, declined at the time to move forward with our plan, as brilliant as it was, he said the company was already exploring a different region. The Middle East was at the time more attractive and many businesses were expanding rapidly to the region. Allan Gray was also thinking of going that route. Nigeria or West Africa would have to come afterwards. The COO did not discard our idea, instead, he set up a task team headed by a more senior white colleague, whose responsibility was to work with my friend and I to delve deeper into our research and come up with even more detailed plans for a potential expansion into Nigeria in the future. I was not interested and felt slighted that my plans were handed over to someone else. Moreover, I did not have forever to wait, I wanted to move back home as soon as possible. It was time to activate the next plan.

The second plan was a little easier. With the help of friends, colleagues, and hours of online research work, I managed to identify two companies that fit the profile of what I wanted. One was a local bank, one of the big four South African banks, and the other, was an international investment bank with offices in South Africa. The interview with the executives of the investment bank went quite well, but unfortunately, they

Unjani Mfwethu?

were still at the early stages of their plans to officially enter the Nigerian market. At that moment, they only serviced the Nigerian market out of the Cape Town office. But they were going to open a Johannesburg office, and wanted to know if I would be willing to consider a role in the Johannesburg office. I did not like the idea. In any case, they wanted to know if I liked rugby as their private clients were big on rugby and the company had a huge rugby sponsorship budget. I declined the offer and we agreed to stay in touch.

The South African bank looked a lot more promising. I had written to the head of their Africa business, who to my delight, had responded positively - copying two of their executives based at the bank's London office. I was invited for a chat, as they called it, in the banks private client building somewhere in Parow, Cape Town. The building was very beautiful, and the furnishings looked luxurious. Not many banks could outshine Allan Gray in this regard, but I was duly impressed. The chat started off on a good note. I decided to be upfront and told them I was planning to relocate to Nigeria and would love to join their team in Nigeria. They explained to me that they were planning to expand to Nigeria, and in fact, the entire West Africa private client. That sounded very good to me, I could see more opportunities opening for me. I had a sense that they were favourably considering my proposal, until it was my turn to ask some questions.

When the three interviewers asked if I had any questions for them, I did not know what exactly to ask, but given that the xenophobic incident that had just happened and was a hot topic nationally at the time, I decided to give it a shot. I asked what the company did for all its foreign nationals during the recent xenophobic attacks - what support was offered and all. I realized from the reactions of the executives that maybe that was not the right question to ask, but it was too late. The three executives looked at one another and were temporarily lost for words. After pondering for a little while, the three confessed that they were not aware of any bank wide efforts in the wake or aftermath of the crisis. If any support was available, they were sure it was probably on a micro level. With regrets on their faces, they asked what my current employer had done. I described how Allan Gray on the day the attack first broke in Cape Town, immediately sent an internal mail to all employees, denouncing the attacks and offering their support in all ways possible to all its foreign national employees. They booked rooms in a nearby hotel for all employees who may be afraid of returning to their respective homes after work and went further to offer transport shuttles. At the end of my speech, the trio looked at me and asked why I would want to leave such a company. It was the end of the interview.

The encounter with the three executives left me rethinking my entire decision up until that moment. I thought about my time at Allan Gray and how truly supportive the company was. The work life balance was not just a buzz word like many other companies. There were numerous measures in place to ensure employee and family cohesion. I grew very quickly within the organization and was exposed to different sides of the business. Working at Allan Gray was indeed a true blessing. Yety's instincts were right the first time back. I pondered if it was a good decision to leave, and even more so, I wondered if it was prudent to leave South Africa for that matter. I wondered if I was being too emotional, perhaps the attack was just a once off, and the South African authorities would ensure that it would never happen again. I was no longer sure if going home was a good idea. It was not like anything had changed back home. The country was still grappling with economic hardships, increasing crime – including sporadic kidnappings and widespread insecurities. Nearly every young person in the country wanted out. I decided to slow down my efforts to leave South Africa a bit, praying that God guides me as He always does.

Sometime in 2010, just a year after the great presentation to my bosses, and the interview with the three executives at the other local bank, I received a call from someone at Standard Bank. He introduced himself as the head of offshore banking at Standard Bank and had received my CV from their Human Resources department. He asked if I was available for coffee sometime in the week. I was very curious and could not wait to find out the details of the call. I had long buried any ambition of leaving Allan Gray or the country.

We met at a café in Claremont and we immediately got into the business of the call. He told me that they were looking at setting up an offshore banking business in West Africa and needed someone to be based permanently in Nigeria. They had tried a brief case approach where someone would fly in from South Africa for few days but was not yielding the desired results. A decision was therefore made to recruit someone who would be based permanently in Nigeria. Their Human Resources managed to pull me out from their database, and he thought I had all the right qualifications. Was I interested in going back home?

What were the odds! I was completely dazed. Just a year back, I was aggressively chasing businesses to give me a chance to go back home, and here I was today, being headhunted by

Unjani Mfwethu?

the biggest bank in Africa. It felt like a dream, and I did not want to wake up from it. Michael asked if I could give my interest in principle, as it would still be a while to finalize the plans. I told him I was interested and happy to wait for them to be ready. I was in no hurry and just a call away.

I did not hear from Michael for months. In the meantime, a lot was happening in my personal life. Yety's mum had developed cancer and had been with us in South Africa for medical treatment. Unfortunately, she did not survive the sickness and passed away in Nigeria sometime mid-March 2011. Her dad suffered a second stroke, consequent to the passing of his wife, and being the only girl, she felt obliged to go home to take care of her dad. Even though the brothers had been doing a great job in her absence, she felt she needed to be with her dad in his difficult moment. For the second time in less than two years, there was an urgency to move back home and that meant I would have to look for a job again.

I remembered Michael and the Standard Bank conversation, so I called him and asked if the job was still available. I told him that there was a family crisis back at home and that I would have to leave for Nigeria urgently, with or without the job. He acted swiftly and told me they were almost concluding negotiations with all parties involved. In the meantime, he would like to start the hiring process in South Africa and wanted me to do a psychometric test. I completed the test, and had two video conference interviews with other executives in the Isle of Man. I received my official letter of employment two weeks after the passing of my mother-in-law, to resume in Nigeria the following month.

When I left Nigeria in 2002, there was minimal South African presence in the country, but by 2011, when I returned home, South African businesses were prevalent in all the sectors of the Nigerian economy. Trade relations between the two countries had increased. With increasing trade and investments, also came increasing movement of people both ways. South African Airways was at some point operating two flights daily from Johannesburg to Lagos. South Africa had become a force in Nigeria, and this had a positive impact on the political relations between the two countries.

Departing South Africa was very emotional. South Africa and its people had been good to me. The country was my refuge when I needed it the most. Its people gave me chance after chance. I have been enriched by its culture and history, and I have kids who are forever tied to South Africa by birth and friends who will remain in my heart forever. I was very grateful for the opportunity to have walked this path, and I returned home with a great sense of fulfilment. Even though this part of my journey may be coming to an end, I knew in my heart that I would always fly the flag of South Africa.

As the resident Offshore Manager for Nigeria and Ghana, I interacted a lot with members of the expatriate community. Naturally, I gravitated towards the South Africa expats the most and they, likewise, were at home with me. They instinctively regarded me as one of them once they got to know my background, even more so, than when I was living in South Africa. But of course, I still had to survive the 'can we trust you' test.

A private banker in South Africa had told me that one of her very good clients, a white guy, had just moved to Nigeria and needed an offshore banking solution. She asked if I could contact him accordingly. I liked easy leads like those. I immediately scheduled an appointment to meet the client and we agreed to meet. I could read the disappointment on his face as soon as I entered the lobby. He probably was not expecting someone that looked like me. I introduced myself, and true to form, he could not hide his disappointment. He asked me directly why the bank would send him a Nigerian. I told him I was the resident Offshore manager and had lived in South Africa for nine years before returning home. The good thing about people like him is that they are quick to understand that somethings are purely transactional, nothing more nothing less.

I did not need to be his friend and he did not have to like me. Without asking for any explanation from him, he went on to tell stories about his previous life in South Africa and his encounter with Nigerians and other Africans. I set up his offshore banking accounts and ended up managing some of his offshore investments. It turned out that he had built some wealth working in Africa for over a decade. At some point, he needed my guidance on an important financial decision. He was having some troubles with his wife and suspected that he might have to go through a divorce. He wanted to know if his assets could be hidden from the wife and her attorneys, and how could I help. Being a Nigerian, I told him that unfortunately, I am unable to help him hide assets. Yes, we provide some level of confidentiality, but only to an extent. We would be obliged to disclose his financial information to any government agency or entities that are authorized to receive such information, for instance the wife's attorney. He was not very happy.

Other than that, I must say I had a very good relationship

Unjani Mfwethu?

with most of the South African Expatriates in Nigeria (all races). We reminisced often about South African politics, crime, and would compare it with the situation in Nigeria. I found that the white South Africans did not seem to miss home as much as the blacks did. In fact, many of the whites seemed to enjoy the Nigerian hospitality. Nigerians have a 'colonial' type reverence for the white. Many of my Nigerian clients would invite my white colleagues over to their homes for dinner, ten times over before inviting me.

Accra, Ghana was even more preferred. Accra is a lot less 'chaotic 'and a lot safer than Lagos. There were some expats who chose to live in Accra, while working in Lagos. I remember meeting a South African mining engineer in Accra. As I approached his residence, I could see two white kids playing outside of the property with the gates widely opened. I waved at the kids as my driver made his way into the compound. The client and I both laughed at the remarkable sight. It was a simple luxury that only South Africans would immediately recognize. They confessed that such freedom and low level of crime was one of the reasons they chose to stay back in the West African country for as long as they could. Indeed, the epidemic of violent crimes was a common theme in conversations with many South African expats and non-South Africans.

I lived about sixty kilometres from the office. We chose to live on the Mainland so we could be close to our parents. This meant that I had to leave home early to avoid the notorious Lagos traffic. On this fateful day, and just mid-way into the journey, I was suddenly awakened from a deep sleep by my driver's scream. When I opened my eyes, I noticed the car was surrounded by gun wielding men. One on the driver's side and two on my side of the vehicle. I was fully awake. I could hear them shouting at me to hand over my laptop bag, wallet, and phones. Unfortunately, I had a substantial amount of money on me, as I had planned to ask my driver to pick up two new tyres for the car once he dropped me off at the office. They took it, as well as my bag, and disappeared into the traffic. No one was hurt. It was ironic, that while I lived in South Africa, I never experienced one incident of crime.

One of the lowest moments of my time back home was during my 'certificate drama' at work. I knew what to expect returning home - all the usual settling in challenges, poor infrastructure and so on. I did not prepare for the level of resistance from my colleagues, my fellow Nigerians. It took organizing individual lunch meetings with some of the 'difficult' colleagues – where I asked directly if they had any problems with me personally, to finally break the ice. But

Unjani Mfwethu?

even that was bearable. What was incomprehensible was the malicious harassment I was subjected to in the name of so called 'routine credential reviews' by Human Resources. This was in my view, the hardest pill to swallow. It was malicious, not because they wanted to conduct a review, but because of the intent, and the way the parties involved went about the exercises. It was malicious because of the pressure they put on the university officials to corroborate their predetermined guilty verdict. It was malicious because of the total disregard for the privacy and reputation of the person being investigated. Again, I was not entirely surprised. But still, it left me mentally and emotionally drained.

I remember standing on the balcony of our apartment in total bewilderment after just receiving the most upsetting call of my entire career. It was a tip off call from a very good friend who had connections inside my bank, even though he was not an employee. He had called to let me know of an ongoing internal investigation by HR around my academic certificates. They seemed to allege that I had not graduated from the University of Lagos as I had claimed. My friend was equally confused. He was a few years my junior at the University of Lagos and had seen me complete my compulsory National Youth Service – a requirement for all Nigerian graduates anywhere in the world. He wanted me to resolve the issue and perhaps, use my family connections at the institution given that my dad was an ex-staff member. It was weird because I had not been officially indicted. I did not know if this was true or some prank.

As I remained in my state of shock, turned anger, Yety, who had heard parts of our telephone conversation, probed to know what the matter was. I did not want to disturb her with such travesty, but after much probing, I gave in. She was livid. She recollected her dad going through a similar experience upon his return from the UK in the 60s with a PhD in Law. She also implored me to pay attention to it. The next few days in the office, I observed certain activities around me that I could link to the tip off I had received earlier. My friend continued to give me updates on the status of the investigation. He notified me that they were waiting desperately on my university to provide them with a corroborative letter before they officially approach me – they were smart. At this point, I was too distressed to concentrate on work. The fact that this was ongoing, was mind boggling, to the extent that I even started to wonder if there was something I was missing. I even had moments of self-doubt – wondering if my certificate and the graduation pictures, were just figments of my imagination. When it seemed like I was starting to second guess myself and losing my mind,

Unjani Mfwethu?

I decided to approach the university myself. The first step was to acquire a particular evidence - which I could only retrieve from the Ghandi library on campus.

I wanted to review the records of my convocation ceremony. I knew that the official ceremonial pamphlet would always list the names of the graduating students and their grades. There was a little challenge. I did not know if I would be allowed access, given I was no longer a student at the university, but I was counting on luck and the fact that I was an alumnus. I should not have been worried. I gained access more easily than I had thought and made my way to the Ghandi section. It was a surreal experience. I had not been in the library building or the Ghandi section in the last sixteen years since I left the university. I looked around and thought how bizarre it was, given that I was back in this revered section of the building under this circumstance. I immediately asked the attendant for the records of the 1995/96 convocation ceremony, and she brought me a copy of the graduation booklet. I could literally hear my heart pounding as I turned the pages of the pamphlet to the faculty of Social Sciences, and the Political Science section. I found my name listed in bold... I inhaled deeply and asked the lady to kindly assist with a copy of the page, and to certify the copy. I had a small sense of what it must feel like to lose one's mind, and the fact that colleagues were inflicting this on me, made me mad!

I thought that since I was on campus anyway, and for good measure, perhaps I should go to the Records Office. I thought I should try, if possible, to view my records onsite as an add-on to what I already had in my possession. I was directed to the office of the Registrar, where I met a lady who later introduced herself as the assistant to the Registrar. She wanted to know how she could be of help as the Registrar was unavailable. I took a seat, looked around a bit – this was familiar grounds to me. The entire university was familiar grounds. I practically grew up at campus and felt comfortable around academic and non-academic staff. I told her I had a hypothetical question and that was, what the procedure was for the verification of a student's certificate or academic records by an external institution. She was intrigued by the question and my demeanour. She wanted to know why I had asked, and I repeated, it was a hypothetical question. She paused, and instead of answering, she asked for my name.

As soon as I mentioned my name, a whole new drama ensued. She immediately jumped up, ran to the adjoining office, and stormed out again with a man. She became hugely animated and asked what God I served. She said my case had

Unjani Mfwethu?

been such a complex one for them. They had been under so much pressure from my employers to provide a letter stating that my certificate was forged, and that I had not completed my studies at the university. I said nothing, all the while fixated on the Registrar. The Registrar said he had just been appointed to the post a month ago and my case would be his first difficult case. When they first received the inquiry from the external consultant acting on behalf of the bank, they had responded that my records showed 'incomplete'. But as soon as they started receiving additional inquiries from the bank, they immediately became a little concerned.

Who was this person that generated so much interest? The lady told me that she cautioned the Registrar and advised that they make their own internal investigation before any further responses to the bank. They had just moved offices some months back, and some of the student files were scattered between the old and the new building. She said she found records of more than two official transcript requests from me in the past, which they had sent to the institutions back then. She said that was evidence that indeed they must have provided my academic records to external parties in the past, but they could not find the academic record or copies of the transcripts sent. I looked in my bag and brought out a copy that I had kept for myself in 2002 when I had requested some for UNISA. The Registrar narrated how they had started digging further, calling on available resources, in the face of mounting pressure from the bank. They told me that they still received a call from my colleagues that morning, asking for the judgement letter from them. They had told them that they needed some more time, but my colleagues had insisted that they needed the letter urgently, and that they would be coming later that afternoon to personally pick up the letter.

All they wanted from the university was a statement stating that I had not completed my studies. The Registrar knew he could not do that given all the dynamics. It baffled them that my employers would be so desperate to convict me. They had never seen anything like it before and wondered what this man must have done to irk the bank. They eventually managed to find my remaining records in a misplaced file in the old building. They also found copies of the complete academic record that they had sent to both UNISA and the Nelson Mandela University where I had obtained a MA in Development Studies in 2009. The most unforgettable part was that they were also unable to verify the certificate that they had issued me. I was mesmerized. The lady told me that if I waited for a few more hours, I would meet them. I was not interested in them, I was even more upset with my university, and its officials because of their sheer inefficiency, would be complicit in the plot to damage the reputation and career of an innocent person. I threatened to sue the university. The Registrar was pleading desperately asking that I should not take any legal actions. I am sure that the university's more recent decision to implement a digital storage system had its roots in my case.

I left the campus on that day with mixed emotions. Even though I was relieved that things unravelled in the manner in which it did, I was saddened that such a reputable university, and arguably the best university in the country, could have dropped the ball. I wondered how many people, without the resources or confidence that I had, would have been destroyed, due to a lack of an efficient and reliable system. I was very angry at the system and wanted desperately to hold people accountable, but I also did not want to be responsible for people's loss of livelihoods. I thought everyone had learnt some valuable lessons and hoped that they would seek to behave better going forward.

I never heard from my HR colleagues. I was later told by a friend and colleague close to HR, that the entire HR hierarchy and my resident supervisor, had debated for days on how to proceed on the matter. All but one executive, wanted to officially indict me, and notify my boss in South Africa. I was told that the dissenting executive insisted that they thread cautiously and try to investigate further before escalating to my boss. Unknowingly to them, I had notified my supervisor about the ongoing allegation the very moment I was tipped off. He advised that we wait patiently and observe how far they would go. He was surprised that the Nigerian subsidiary would assume that they would employ someone whom they had not vetted themselves.

Years after I had left the bank, I ran into the 'dissenting executive'. I could not resist the temptation to ask why he took a different stance to his colleagues in the certificate fraud drama. He was at first shocked that I was aware of the entire investigation. He told me that his major concern at the time was that the story did not add up. He just had a feeling that something was amiss, and he was not the one to let sentiments override his judgements, especially when it came to professional matters.

It is sad that we often let our emotions cloud our sense of good judgements in our dealings with people. While it is true that there are a growing number of certificate frauds in Nigeria and globally too, it is important that every case be considered on its own merits or demerits.

Unjani Mfwethu?

In this case, one individual was able to put aside his emotions, ignoring the noise around him so he could ask pertinent questions to interrogate the logic of their allegations. He wanted to understand why someone who had committed fraud would return ceremoniously to the same country with his family, and more importantly, did his previous employers and institutions of higher learnings in South Africa, not conduct background checks on him? Others allowed themselves to be consumed by some nefarious motives, to the extent that they ignored all sense of reason. I was back in my country. These were my own people. I was supposed to feel more at home, but it sure did not feel like it. It does not matter who we are, where we are from or where we live, we will always be faced with challenges and prejudices. It is our ability, both as leaders and ordinary people, to rise above sentiments in our dealings, that sets us apart.

If we are to build a society that loves rather than hates, that listens more than it hears, that builds up rather than tears down, that embraces rather than discards, each one of us in our little corners and spheres of influence, will have to play our part. Let us start by taking a moment to notice the other.

EPILOGUE

I had to wake up early after an exhausting dinner with members of the Golden Key Club. Herb and I drove to the Winter Haven campus in his new Nissan SUV. The first of my five-day lecture at Polk State University, Florida, would be starting that morning at 10h00. It was humbling to see posters of the annual International Student week with my pictures on it, adorning the walls of the campus.

I met Professor Herb Nold in 2013, during the Academy of Management Conference in Orlando, Florida. We both attended a 'breakaway session' on Africa. I had arrived much earlier, and few minutes before the start of the program, I saw a 'geek' looking white male walk into the conference room looking very lost. He was one of the few whites that were present in the room. He quickly scanned the room and made his way to my table.

Later that year, he visited Cape Town along with a handful of his students on an educational tour of South Africa. He reached out to me upon his arrival, and asked if I could meet his students, and share some experiences as well as advise on places of interest to visit. One thing led to another, and I became a regular guest speaker at his university, Polk State College in Florida. I spoke on several 'Africa and Business ethics' related topics. It was an area we were both passionate about.

During one of the lectures, I remember an African American student asking me how I had managed to overcome many of the challenges I described in my lecture. It was an appropriate question given the similarities in the systemic challenges facing the black person anywhere in the world. I smiled and acknowledged that while it may appear that a significant stride has been achieved through the grace of God, there remain many more mountains to climb.

It was December 2014, we had just moved to Pretoria from Cape Town at the beginning of the year, to start a new job in Pretoria. December is a usually quiet time of the year in Pretoria as most of the population would have left the city for their respective holiday destinations along the coast or abroad. It was always a good time to enjoy some peace and quiet, and less traffic. My wife wanted to do some Christmas shopping and I thought it might be a good opportunity to look around. Mid-way into our shopping experience, I was approached by a young man who identified himself as a student of the University of Pretoria. Given my background and history in the country, I always made sure to give audience to anyone who may appear to be selling something or conducting a survey - no matter how inconvenient it may be. The young man happened to be conducting a survey for the retail industry. He asked a variety of questions targeted around my shopping habits, and towards the end of the survey, asked for my income bracket. I noticed on his handheld device that there were about four categories for monthly income levels: <R10, 000; R10, 000 –R20, 000; R20, 000-R40, 000, and >R40, 000. I selected the last option. The young student looked at me again. I could tell that he probably thought I was mistaken. He repeated that it was a monthly income level, and I told him that I understood the question very well. He was even more confused. He asked which industry I worked in, and I told him I was a banker. He was starting to recover from his shock. I asked what he was studying, and he told me he was an engineering student. I told him to stick to it. He has a higher chance of making more money than I could. As I walked away, I could see him run across to his friends, and shared his discovery.

I walked up to my wife and kids who were by now wondering where I had disappeared to. She asked why I had a grin on my face. I smiled broadly and told her that the strangest thing just happened to me.

Unjani Mfwethu?